THE
HISTORY OF PHILOSOPHY
IN ISLAM

THE
HISTORY OF PHILOSOPHY
IN ISLAM

By

DR. T. J. DE BOER

Translated by

EDWARD R. JONES, B.D.

DOVER PUBLICATIONS, INC.
NEW YORK

Published in Canada by General Publishing Company, Ltd., 30 Lesmill Road, Don Mills, Toronto, Ontario.

Published in the United Kingdom by Constable and Company, Ltd., 10 Orange Street, London WC 2.

This Dover edition, first published in 1967, is an unabridged and unaltered republication of the work originally published by Luzac & Co., in 1903.

Standard Book Number: 486-21754-X
Library of Congress Catalog Card Number: 66-30424

Manufactured in the United States of America
Dover Publications, Inc.
180 Varick Street
New York, N. Y. 10014

TRANSLATOR'S PREFATORY NOTE.

This edition of Dr. DE BOER's recent work is produced in the hope that it may prove interesting to not a few English readers, and especially that it may be of service to younger students commencing to study the subject which is dealt with in the following pages. The translator has aimed at nothing more than a faithful reproduction of the original. His best thanks are due to the accomplished author, for his kindness in revising the proof-sheets of the version, as it passed through the Press.

E. R. J.

PREFACE.

The following is the first attempt which has been made, since the appearance of Munk's excellent sketch [1], to present in connected form a History of Philosophy in Islam. This work of mine may therefore be regarded as a fresh initiation, — not a completion of such a task. I could not know of all that had been done by others, in the way of preliminary study in this field; and when I did know of the existence of such material, it was not always accessible to me. As for manuscript assistance, it was only in exceptional cases that this was at my disposal.

Conforming to the conditions which I had to meet, I have in the following account refrained from stating my authorities. But anything which I may have taken over, nearly word for word or without testing it, I have marked in foot-references. For the rest, I deeply regret that I cannot duly indicate at present how much I owe, as regards appreciation of the sources, to men like Dieterici, de Goeje, Goldziher, Houtsma, Aug. Müller, Munk, Nöldeke, Renan, Snouck Hurgronje, van Vloten, and many, many others.

Since the completion of this volume an interesting monograph on Ibn Sina [2] has appeared, which farther extends

---

[1] S. MUNK, "*Mélanges de Philosophie juive et arabe*", Paris 1859.
[2] CARRA DE VAUX, "*Avicenne*", Paris 1900.

its survey over the earlier history of Philosophy in Islam. It gives rise to no occasion, however, to alter substantially my conception of the subject.

For all bibliographical details I refer the reader to "die Orientalische Bibliographie", Brockelmann's "Geschichte der Arabischen Litteratur", and Ueberweg—Heinze's "Grundriss der Geschichte der Philosophie" II³, p. 213 *sqq*. In the transcription of Arabic names I have been more heedful of tradition and German pronunciation, than of consistency. Be it noted only that *z* is to be pronounced as a soft *s*, and *th* like the corresponding English sound [1]. In the Index of Personal Names, accents signify length.

As far as possible I have confined myself to Islam. On that ground Ibn Gebirol and Maimonides have received only a passing notice, while other Jewish thinkers have been entirely omitted, although, philosophically considered, they belong to the Muslim school. This, however, entails no great loss, for much has been written already about the Jewish philosophers, whereas Muslim thinkers have hitherto been sadly neglected.

Groningen (Netherlands).

T. J. DE BOER.

---

[1] [*Translator's Note:* In this version the transliteration has been adapted as far as possible to English sounds].

CONTENTS.

CHAPTER I.

INTRODUCTION.

CHAPTER II.

Philosophy and Arab Knowledge.

CHAPTER III.

The Pythagorean Philosophy.

CHAPTER IV.

The Neo-Platonic Aristotelians of The East.

CHAPTER V.

THE OUTCOME OF PHILOSOPHY IN THE EAST.

CHAPTER VI.

PHILOSOPHY IN THE WEST.

I. INTRODUCTION.

1. THE THEATRE.

1. In olden time the Arabian desert was, as it is at this day, the roaming-ground of independent Bedouin tribes. With free and healthy minds they contemplated their monotonous world, whose highest charm was the raid, and whose intellectual treasure was the tribal tradition. Neither the achievements of social labour, nor the accomplishments of elegant leisure were known to them. Only on the borders of the desert, in regularly constituted communities, which often had to suffer from the incursions of those Bedouins, a higher degree of civilization had been attained. This was the case in the South, where the ancient kingdom of the Queen of Sheba continued its existence in Christian times under Abyssinian or Persian overlordship. On the West lay Mecca and Medina (Yathrib), by an old caravan route; and Mecca in particular, with its market safe-guarded by a temple, was the centre of a brisk traffic. Lastly on the North, two semi-sovereign States had been formed under Arab princes: towards Persia, the kingdom of the Lakhmids in Hira; and towards Byzantium the dominion of the Gassanids in Syria. In speech and poetry, however, the unity of the Arab nation was set forth to some extent

even before Mohammed's time. The poets were the 'men of knowledge' for their people. Their incantations held good as oracles, first of all for their several tribes, but no doubt extending their influence often beyond their own particular septs.

2. Mohammed and his immediate successors, Abu Bekr, Omar, Othman and Ali (622—661) succeeded in inspiring the free sons of the desert, together with the more civilized inhabitants of the coast-lands, with enthusiasm for a joint enterprise. To this circumstance Islam owes its world-position: for Allah showed himself great, and the world was quite small for those who surrendered themselves to him (Muslims). In a short time the whole of Persia was conquered, and the East-Roman empire lost its fairest provinces, — Syria and Egypt.

Medina was the seat of the first Caliphs or representatives of the prophet. Then Mohammed's brave son-in-law Ali, and Ali's sons, fell before Moawiya, the able governor of Syria. From that time dates the existence of the party of Ali (Shi'ites), which in the course of diverse vicissitudes, — now reduced to subjection, now in detached places attaining power, — lives on in history, until it finally incorporates itself with the Persian kingdom in definite opposition to Sunnite Islam.

In their struggle against the secular power the Shi'ites availed themselves of every possible weapon, — even of science. Very early there appears among them the sect of the Kaisanites, which ascribes to Ali and his heirs a superhuman secret lore, by the help of which the inner meaning of the Divine revelation first becomes clear, but which demands from its devotees not less faith in, and absolute obedience to, the possessor of such knowledge, than does the letter of the Koran. (Cf. III, 2 § 1).

3. After the victory of Moawiya, who made Damascus the capital of the Muslim empire, the importance of Medina lay mainly in the spiritual province. It had to content itself with fostering, partly under Jewish and Christian influences, a knowledge of the Law and Tradition. In Damascus, on the other hand, the Omayyads (661—750) conducted the secular government. Under their rule the empire spread from the Atlantic to districts beyond the frontiers of India and Turkestan, and from the Indian Ocean to the Caucasus and the very walls of Constantinople. With this development, however, it had reached its farthest extension.

Arabs now assumed everywhere the leading position. They formed a military aristocracy; and the most striking proof of their influence is the fact, that conquered nations with an old and superior civilization accepted the language of their conquerors. Arabic became the language of Church and State, of Poetry and Science. But while the higher offices in the State and the Army were administered by Arabs in preference, the care of the Arts and Sciences fell, first of all, to Non-Arabs and men of mixed blood. In Syria school-instruction was received from Christians. The chief seats of intellectual culture, however, were Basra and Kufa, in which Arabs and Persians, Muslims, Christians, Jews and Magians rubbed shoulders together. There, where trade and industry were thriving, the beginnings of secular science in Islam must be sought for, — beginnings themselves due to Hellenistic-Christian and Persian influences.

4. The Omayyads were succeeded by the Abbasids

(750—1258). To obtain the sovereignty, the latter had granted concessions to the Persians, and had utilized religio-political movements. During the first century of their rule (i. e. up to about 860), though only during that period, the greatness of the empire continued to increase, or at least it held its own. In the year 762, Mansur, the second ruler of this house, founded Bagdad as the new capital, — a city which soon outshone Damascus in worldly splendour, and Basra and Kufa in intellectual illumination. Constantinople alone could be compared to it. Poets and scholars, particularly from the North-Eastern provinces, met together in Bagdad at the court of Mansur (754—775), of Harun (786—809), of Mamun (813—833), and others. Several of the Abbasids had a liking for secular culture, whether for its own sake or to adorn their court, and although they may often have failed to recognize the value of artists and learned men, these at any rate could appreciate the material benefits conferred upon them by their patrons.

From the time of Harun at least, there existed in Bagdad a library and a learned institute. Even under Mansur, but especially under Mamun and his successors, translation of the scientific literature of the Greeks into the Arabic tongue went forward, largely through the agency of Syrians; and Abstracts and Commentaries bearing upon these works were also composed.

Just when this learned activity was at its highest, the glory of the empire began to decline. The old tribal feuds, which had never been at rest under the Omayyads, had seemingly given place to a firmly-knit political unity; but other controversies, — theological and metaphysical wranglings, such as in like manner accompanied the decay of the East-Roman empire, — were prosecuted with ever-increasing bitterness. The service of the State, under an Eastern despotism, did not require men of brilliant parts. Promising abilities accordingly were often ruined in luxurious indulgence, or flung away upon sophistry and the show of learning. On the other hand, for the defence of the empire the Caliphs enlisted the sound and healthy vigour of nations who had not been so much softened by over-civilization, — first the Iranian or Iranianized people of Khorasan, and then the Turks.

5. The decline of the empire became more and more evident. The power of the Turkish soldiery, uprisings of city mobs and of peasant labourers, Shi'ite and Ismaelite intrigues on all sides, and in addition the desire for independence shown by the distant provinces, — were either the causes or the symptoms of the downfall. Alongside of the Caliphs, who were reduced to the position of spiritual dignitaries, the Turks ruled as Mayors of the Palace; and all round, in the outlying regions of the empire, independent States were gradually formed, until an utterly astounding body of minor States appeared. The most influential ruling houses, more or less independent, were the following: in the West, to say nothing of the Spanish Omayyads (cf. VI, 1), the Aglabids of North Africa, the Tulunids and Fatimids of Egypt, and the Hamdanids of Syria and Mesopotamia; in the East, The Tahirids and Samanids, who were by slow degrees supplanted by the Turks. It is at the courts of these petty dynasties that the poets and scholars of the next period (the 10th and 11th centuries) are to be found. For a short time Haleb (Aleppo), the seat of the Hamdanids, and for a longer

time Cairo, built by the Fatimids in the year 969, — have a better claim to be regarded as the home of intellectual endeavour than Bagdad itself. For another brief space lustre is shed on the East by the court of the Turk, Mahmud of Ghazna, who had become master of Khorasan in the year 999.

The founding of the Muslim Universities also falls within this period of petty States and Turkish administration. The first one was erected in Bagdad in the year 1065; and from that date the East has been in possession of Science, but only in the form of stereotyped republications. The teacher conveys the teaching which has been handed down to him by his teachers; and in any new book hardly a sentence will be found which does not appear in older books. Science was rescued from danger; but the learned men of Transoxiana, who, upon hearing of the establishment of the first Madrasah, appointed a solemn memorial service, as tradition tells, to be held in honour of departed science, have been shewn to be correct in their estimate. [1]

Then, — in the 13th century, — there came storming over the Eastern regions of Islam the resounding invasion of the Mongols, who swept away whatever the Turks had spared. No culture ever flourished there again, to develope from its own resources a new Art or to stimulate a revival of Science.

2. ORIENTAL WISDOM.

1. Prior to its contact with Hellenism, the Semitic mind had proceeded no farther in the path of Philosophy than the propounding of enigmas, and the utterance of apho-

[1] *Cf.* Snouck Hurgronje, "Mekka", II, p. 228 *sq.*

ristic wisdom. Detached observations of Nature, but especially of the life and fate of Man, form the basis of such thinking; and where comprehension ceases, resignation to the almighty and inscrutable will of God comes in without difficulty. We have become familiar with this kind of wisdom from the Old Testament; and that it was developed in like manner among the Arabs, is shewn to us by the Bible story of the Queen of Sheba, and by the figure of the wise Loqman in the Arab tradition.

By the side of this wisdom there was found everywhere the Magic of the sorcerer, — a knowledge which was authenticated by command over outward things. But it was only in the priestly circles of ancient Babylonia, — under what influences and to what extent we do not precisely know, — that men rose to a more scientific consideration of the world. Their eyes were turned from the confusion of earthly existence to the order of the heavens. They were not like the Hebrews, who never got beyond the wondering stage [1], or who saw merely an emblem of their own posterity in the countless stars [2]; they resembled rather the Greeks who came to understand the Many and the Manifold in their sublunary forms, only after they had discovered the harmony of the All in the unity and steadiness of the movement of the heavens. The only drawback was that much mythological by-play and astrological pretence was interwoven with what was good, as in fact was the case also in Hellenism. This Chaldaean wisdom, from the time of Alexander the Great, became pervaded, in Babylonia and Syria, with Hellenistic and later with Hellenistic-Christian ideas, or else was supplanted by them.

[1] Job XXXVIII.   [2] Gen. XV : 5.

In the Syrian city of Harran only, up to the time of Islam, the old heathenism held its ground, little affected by Christian influences. (Cf. I, 3, § 4).

2. Of more importance than any Semitic tradition, was the contribution made to Islam by Persian and Indian wisdom. We do not need to enter here upon the question as to whether Oriental wisdom was originally influenced by Greek philosophy, or Greek philosophy by Oriental wisdom. What Islam carried away directly from Persians and Indians may be learned with tolerable certainty from Arabic sources, and to this we may confine ourselves.

Persia is the land of Dualism, and it is not improbable that its dualistic religious teaching exercised an influence upon theological controversy in Islam, either directly or through the Manichaeans and other Gnostic sects. But much greater, in worldly circles, was the influence wielded by that system which, according to tradition, came to be even publicly recognized, under the Sasanid Yezdegerd II (438/9—457), viz. Zrwanism (Cf. III, 1, § 6). In this system the dualistic view of the world was superseded by setting up endless Time, (*zrwan*, Arab. *dahr*) as the paramount principle, and identifiying it with Fate, the outermost heavenly sphere or the movement of the heavens. This doctrine, pleasing to philosophic intellects, has secured, with or without the guise of Islam, a prominent place for itself in Persian literature and in the views of the people, up to our own day. By theologians, however, and no less by philosophers of the Idealistic schools, it was disavowed as Materialism, Atheism and so forth.

3. India was regarded as the true land of wisdom. In Arab writers we often come upon the view that there the

birthplace of philosophy is to be found. By peaceful trading, in which the agents between India and the West were principally Persians, and next as a result of the Muslim conquest, acquaintance with Indian wisdom spread far and wide. Much of it was translated under Mansur (754—775) and Harun (786—809), partly by means of the intervening step of Persian (Pahlawi) versions, and partly from the Sanskrit direct. Many a deliverance of ethical and political wisdom, in the dress of proverbs, was taken over from the fables and tales of India, such as the Tales of the Pantshatantra, translated from the Pahlawi by Ibn al-Muqaffa in Mansur's time, and others. It was, however, Indian Mathematics and Astrology, — the latter in combination with practical Medicine and Magic, — that mainly influenced the beginnings of secular wisdom in Islam. The Astrology of the Siddhanta of Brahmagupta, which was translated from the Sanskrit, under Mansur, by Fazari assisted by Indian scholars, was known even before Ptolemy's Almagest. A wide world, past and future, was thereby opened up. The high figures with which the Indians worked produced a powerful, perplexing impression upon the sober Muslim annalists, just as, on the other hand, Arab merchants, who in India and China put the age of our created world at a few thousand years, exposed themselves to the utmost ridicule.

Nor did the logical and metaphysical speculations of the Indians remain unknown to the Muslims. These produced, however, much less effect on scientific development than did their Mathematics and Astrology. The investigations of the Indians, associated with their sacred books and wholly determined by a religious purpose, have certainly had a lasting influence upon Persian Sufism and Islamic Mysticism. But, — once for all, — Philosophy is a Greek conception, and we have no right, in deference to the taste of the day, to allot an undue amount of space in our description to the childish thoughts of pious Hindoos. What has been advanced by these meditative penitents about the deceptive show of everything sensuous, may often possess a poetic charm, just as it agrees perhaps with those observations on the evanescence of all that is earthly, which the East had access to in Neo-Pythagorean and Neo-Platonic sources; but it has contributed just as little of importance as these did, towards the explanation of phenomena or the awakening of the scientific spirit. Not the Indian imagination, but the Greek mind was needed to direct the reflective process to the knowledge of the Real. The best example of this is furnished by Arabic Mathematics. In the opinion of those who know the subject best, almost the only thing Indian in it is the Arithmetic, while the Algebra and the Geometry are Greek, preponderatingly, if not exclusively. Hardly a single Indian penetrated to the notion of pure mathematics. Number, even in its highest form, remained always something concrete; and in Indian Philosophy knowledge in the main continued to be only a means. Deliverance from the evil of existence was the aim, and Philosophy a pathway to the life of blessedness. Hence the monotony of this wisdom, — concentrated, as it was, upon the essence of all things in its One-ness, — as contrasted with the many-branched science of the Hellenes, which strove to comprehend the operations of Nature and Mind on all sides.

Oriental wisdom, Astrology and Cosmology delivered over

to Muslim thinkers material of many kinds, but the Form,
— the formative principle, — came to them from the Greeks.
In every case where it is not mere enumeration or chance
concatenation that is taken in hand, but where an attempt
is made to arrange the Manifold according to positive or
logical points of view, we may conclude with all probability that Greek influences have been at work.

3. GREEK SCIENCE.

1. Just as the commercial intercourse between India and
China and Byzantium was conducted principally by the
Persians, so in the remote West, as far even as France,
the Syrians came forward as the agents of civilization. It
was Syrians who brought wine, silk &c. to the West.
But it was Syrians also who took Greek culture from
Alexandria and Antioch, spreading it eastward and pro-
pagating it in the schools of Edessa and Nisibis, Harran
and Gondeshapur. Syria was the true neutral ground, where
for centuries the two world-powers, the Roman and the
Persian, came in contact with one another, either as friends
or as foes. In such circumstances, the Christian Syrians
played a part similar to the one which in later days fell
to the share of the Jews.

2. The Muslim conquerors found the Christian church
split up into three main divisions, — to say nothing of
many sects. The Monophysite church, alongside of the
Orthodox State-church, preponderated in Syria proper, and
the Nestorian church in Persia. The difference between the
doctrinal systems of these churches was perhaps not without
importance for the development of Muslim Dogmatics. Ac-

cording to the teaching of the Monophysites, God and Man were united in *one* nature in Christ, whereas the Orthodox, and in a still more pronounced manner the Nestorians, discriminated between a Divine nature and a human nature in him. Now nature means, above everything, energy or operative principle. The question, accordingly, which is at issue, is whether the Divine, and the human Willing and Acting are one and the same in Christ or different. The Monophysites, from speculative and religious motives, gave prominence to the Unity in Christ their God, at the expense of the human element: The Nestorians, on the other hand, emphasized, in contrast with the Divine element, all that is specially characteristic of human Being, Willing and Acting. The latter view, however, favoured by political circumstances and conditions of culture, offers freer play to philosophical speculations on the world and on life. In point of fact the Nestorians did most for the cultivation of Greek Science.

Syriac was the language both of the Western and of the Eastern or Persian Church; but Greek was also taught along with it in the Cloister schools. Rasain and Kinnesrin must be mentioned as being centres of culture in the Western or Monophysite Church. Of more importance, at the outset at least, was the school of Edessa, inasmuch as the dialect of Edessa had risen to the position of the literary language; but in the year 489 the school there was closed because of the Nestorian views held by its teachers. It was then re-opened in Nisibis, and, being patronized by the Sasanids on political grounds, it disseminated Nestorian belief and Greek knowledge throughout Persia.

Instruction in these schools had a pre-eminently Biblical and ecclesiastical character, and was arranged to meet the needs of the Church. However, physicians or coming students of medicine also took part in it. The circumstance that they frequently belonged to the ecclesiastical order does not do away with the distinction between theological study and the pursuit of secular knowledge. It is true that according to the Syro-Roman code, Teachers (learned Priests) and Physicians were entitled in common to exemption from taxation and to other privileges; but the very fact that priests were regarded as healers of the soul, while physicians had merely to patch up the body, seemed to justify the precedence accorded to the former. Medicine always remained a secular matter; and, by the regulations of the School of Nisibis (from the year 590), the Holy Scriptures were not to be read in the same room with books that dealt with worldly callings.

In medical circles the works of Hippocrates, Galen and Aristotle were highly prized; but in the cloisters Philosophy was understood to be first of all the contemplative life of the ascetic, and "the one thing needful" was the only thing cared for.

4. The Mesopotamian city of Harran, in the neighbourhood of Edessa, takes a place of its own. In this city, especially when it began to flourish again after the Arab conquest, ancient Semitic paganism comes into association with mathemathical and astronomical studies and Neo-Pythagorean and Neo-Platonic speculation. The Harranaeans or Sabacans, as they were called in the 9th and 10th centuries, traced their mystic lore back to Hermes Trismegistus, Agathodaemon, Uranius and others. Numerous pseud-

epigraphs of the later Hellenism were adopted by them in good faith, and some perhaps were forged in their own circle. A few of them became active as translators and learned authors, and many kept up a brisk scientific intercourse with Persian and Arab scholars from the 8th to the 10th century.

5. In Persia, at Gondeshapur, we find an Institution for philosophical and medical studies established by Khosrau Anosharwan (521—579). Its teachers were principally Nestorian Christians; but Khosrau, who had an inclination for secular culture, extended his toleration to Monophysites as well as to Nestorians. At that time, just as was the case later at the court of the Caliphs, Christian Syrians were held in special honour as medical men.

Farther, in the year 529, seven philosophers of the Neo-Platonic school, who had been driven away from Athens, found a place of refuge at the court of Khosrau. Their experiences there, however, may have resembled those of the French free-thinkers of the 18th century at the Russian court. At all events they longed to get home again; and the king was sufficiently liberal-minded and magnanimous to allow them to go, and in his treaty of peace with Byzantium of the year 549 to stipulate in their case for freedom of religious opinion. Their stay in the Persian kingdom was doubtless not wholly devoid of influence.

6. The period of Syriac translations of profane literature from the Greek extends perhaps from the 4th to the 8th century. In the 4th century collections of aphorisms were translated. The first translator, however, who makes his appearance avowing his name, is Probus, "Priest and physician in Antioch" (1st half of the 5th century?). Possibly

he was merely an expounder of the logical writings of Aristotle, and of the Isagoge of Porphyry. Better known is Sergius of Rasain, — who died at the age of 70 or so, probably in Constantinople, about 536, — a Mesopotamian monk and physician, whose studies, which were probably pursued in Alexandria itself, took in the whole range of Alexandrian science, and whose translations not only embraced Theology, Morals and Mysticism, but even Physics, Medicine and Philosophy. Even after the Muslim conquest the learned activity of the Syrians continued. Jacob of Edessa (*circa* 640—708) translated Greek theological writings; but he occupied himself besides with Philosophy, and in answer to a question relative thereto he pronounced that it was lawful for Christian ecclesiastics to impart the higher instruction to children of Muslim parents. There was thus a felt need of culture among the latter.

The translations of the Syrians, particularly of Sergius of Rasain, are generally faithful; but a more exact correspondence with the original is shewn in the case of Logic and Natural Science than in Ethical and Metaphysical works. Much that is obscure in these last has been misunderstood or simply omitted, and much that is pagan has been replaced by Christian material. For instance, Peter, Paul and John would come upon the scene in room of Socrates, Plato and Aristotle. Destiny and the Gods were obliged to give place to the one God; and ideas like World, Eternity, Sin and the like were recast in a Christian mould. The Arabs, however, in subsequent times went to a much greater length with the process of adaptation to their language, culture and religion than the Syrians. This may perhaps be partly explained by the Muslim horror of everything heathen, but partly too by their greater faculty of adaptation.

7. Apart from a few mathematical, physical and medical writings, the Syrians interested themselves in two subjects, — the *first* consisting of moralizing collections of aphorisms, put together into a kind of history of Philosophy, and, generally, of mystical Pythagorean-Platonic wisdom. This is found principally in pseudepigraphs, which bear the names of Pythagoras, Socrates, Plutarch, Dionysius and others. The centre of interest is a Platonic doctrine of the Soul, subjected to a later Pythagorean, Neo-Platonic, or Christian form of treatment. In the Syrian cloisters Plato is even turned into an oriental monk, who built a cell for himself in the heart of the wilderness, far away from the dwellings of men, and after three years' silent brooding over a verse of the Bible was led to a recognition of the Tri-Unity of God.

A *second* subject of interest was added, in Aristotle's Logic. Among the Syrians, and for a longer period among the Arabs also, Aristotle was commonly known almost solely as a logician. This knowledge, just as in the early scholasticism of the West, extended to the Categories, the Hermeneutics, and the first Analytics as far as the Categorical Figures. They stood in need of the Logic in order to comprehend the writings of Greek ecclesiastical teachers, since these, at least in form, were influenced thereby. But as they did not possses it complete, as little did they possess it pure. They had it before them only in a Neo-Platonic redaction, as may be seen, for example, from the work of Paulus Persa, which was written in Syriac for Khosrau Anosharwan. In that work knowledge is placed above faith, and philosophy is defined as the process by which the soul becomes conscious of its own inner essence, in which, like a God as it were, it sees all things.

8. What the Arabs owe to the Syrians is expressed by this circumstance amongst others, — that Arab scholars held Syriac to be the oldest, or the real (natural) language. The Syrians, it is true, produced nothing original; but their activity as translators was of advantage to Arab-Persian science. It was Syrians almost without exception, who, from the 8th century to the 10th, rendered Greek works into Arabic, either from the older Syriac versions or from those which had been in part improved by them, and in part re-arranged. Even the Omayyad prince, Khalid ibn Yezid (died 704), who occupied himself with Alchemy under the guidance of a Christian monk, is said to have provided for translations of works on Alchemy from Greek into Arabic. Proverbs, maxims, letters, wills, and in short whatever bore on the history of philosophy, were at a very early time collected and translated. But it was not till the reign of Mansur that a commencement was made with the translation into Arabic — partly from Pahlawi versions — of those writings of the Greeks which deal with Natural Science, Medicine and Logic. Ibn al-Moqaffa, an adherent of Persian Dualism, took a leading part in this task, from whom later workers must have marked themselves off by their terminology. None of his philosophical translations have come down to us. Other material too, belonging to the 8th century has gone amissing. The earliest specimen of this work of translation which we possess dates from the 9th century, the time of Mamun and his successors.

The translators of the 9th century were, for the most

part, medical men; and Hippocrates and Galen were among
the first to be translated after Ptolemy and Euclid. But
let us confine ourselves to Philosophy, in the narrower sense.
A translation of the Timäus of Plato is said to have come
from Yuhanna or Yakhya ibn Bitriq (in the beginning of
the 9th century), as well as Aristotle's 'Meteorology', the
'Book of Animals', an epitome of the 'Psychology', and
the tract 'On the World'. To Abdalmasikh ibn Abdallah
Naima al-Himsi (*circa* 835) is to be ascribed a rendering
of the 'Sophistics' of Aristotle, in addition to the Commentary of John Philoponus upon the 'Physics', as well as the
so-called 'Theology of Aristotle', — a paraphrased epitome
of the Enneads of Plotinus. Qosta ibn Luqa al-Balabakki
(*circa* 835) is said to have translated the Commentaries of
Alexander of Aphrodisias and John Philoponus upon the
'Physics' of Aristotle, and in part, Alexander's Commentary
on the 'De generatione et corruptione', as well as the 'Pla-
cita Philosophorum' of the Pseudo-Plutarch, and other works.

The most productive translators were Abu Zaid Honain
ibn Ishaq (809?—873), his son, Ishaq ibn Honain († 910
or 911), and nephew Hobaish ibn al-Hasan. Seeing that
they worked together, there is a good deal which is
ascribed, now to the one and now to the other. Not a little
material must have been prepared, under their oversight,
by disciples and subordinates. Their activity extended over
the whole range of the science of that day. Existing translations were improved, and new ones added. The father
preferred to work at versions of medical authors, but the
son turned more to the rendering of philosophical material.

The work of the translators was still proceeding in the
10th century. Among those who especially distinguished

themselves were Abu Bishr Matta ibn Yunus al-Qannai († 940), Abu Zakarya Yakhya ibn Adi al-Mantiqi († 974), Abu Ali Isa ibn Ishaq ibn Zura († 1008), and finally, Abu-l-Khair al-Hasan ibn al-Khammar (born 942), a pupil of Yakhya ibn Adi's, of whose writings, besides translations, commentaries, and so forth, a tract is mentioned, on the Harmony between Philosophy and Christianity.

From the time of Honain ibn Ishaq the activity of the translators was almost wholly confined to Aristotelian and Pseudo-Aristotelian writings, and to epitomes of them, to paraphrases of their contents and to commentaries upon them.

9. These translators are not to be regarded as specially great philosophers. Their work was seldom entered upon spontaneously, but almost always at the command of some Caliph or Vizir or other person of note. Outside of their own department of study, usually Medicine, they were chiefly interested in Wisdom, — that is, in pretty stories with a moral, in anecdotes, and in oracular sayings. The expressions which we merely bear with in intercourse, in narrative or on the stage, as being characteristic utterances with certain persons, were admired and collected by these worthy people for the sake of the wisdom contained in them, or perhaps even for no more than the rhetorical elegance of their form. As a rule, those men continued true to the Christian faith of their fathers. The traditional story of Ibn Djebril gives a good idea both of their way of thinking and of the liberal-mindedness of the Caliphs. When Mansur wanted to convert him to Islam, he is said to have replied: "In the faith of my fathers I will die: where they are, I wish also to be, whether in heaven or

in hell". Whereupon the Caliph laughed, and dismissed him with a rich present.

Only a small portion has been saved of the original writings of these men. A short dissertation by Qosta ibn Luqa on the distinction between Soul and Spirit ($\pi\nu\varepsilon\tilde{\upsilon}\mu\alpha$, *ruh*), preserved in a Latin translation, has been frequently mentioned and made use of. According to it, the Spirit is a subtle material, which from its seat in the left ventricle of the heart animates the human frame and brings about its movements and perceptions. The finer and clearer this Spirit is, the more rationally the man thinks and acts: there is but one opinion upon this point. It is more difficult, however, to predicate anything sure, and universally valid, of the Soul. The deliverances of the greatest philosophers occasionally differ, and occasionally contradict each other. In any case the Soul is incorporeal, for it adopts qualities, and, in fact, qualities of the most opposite nature at one and the same time. It is uncompounded and unchangeable, and it does not, like the Spirit, perish with the body. The Spirit only acts as an intermediary between the Soul and the Body, and it is in this way that it becomes a secondary cause of movement and perception.

The statement which has just been given regarding the Soul is found in many of the later writers. But by slow degrees, as the Aristotelian philosophy thrusts Platonic opinions more and more into the background, another pair of opposites come into full view. Physicians alone continue to speak of the importance of the *'ruh'* or Spirit of Life. Philosophers institute a comparison between Soul and Spirit or Reason ($\nu o\tilde{\upsilon}\varsigma$, *'aql*). The Soul is now reduced to the domain of the perishable, and sometimes, in Gnostic fashion, even

to the lower and evil realm of the desires. The rational
Spirit, — as that which is highest, that which is imperishable in man — is exalted above the Soul.

In this notice, however, we are anticipating history: let
us return to our translators.

10. The most valuable portion of the legacy which the
Greek mind bequeathed to us in art, poetry, and historical
composition, was never accessible to the Orientals. It would
even have been difficult for them to understand it, seeing
that they lacked the due acquaintance with Greek life,
and the relish for it. For them the history of Greece began
with Alexander the Great, surrounded with the halo of
legend; and the position which Aristotle held beside the
greatest prince of ancient times must have assuredly con-
duced to the acceptance of the Aristotelian philosophy at
the Muslim court. Arab historians counted up the Greek
princes, on to Cleopatra, and then the Roman Emperors;
but a Thucydides, for example, was not known to them,
even by name. Of Homer they had not picked up much
more than the sentence, that "one only should be the
ruler". They had not the least idea of the great Greek
dramatists and lyric poets. It was only through its
Mathematics, Natural Science and Philosophy, that Greek
antiquity could bring its influence to bear upon them.
They had come to know something of the development
of Greek Philosophy, from Plutarch, Porphyry and others,
as well as from the writings of Aristotle and Galen. A
good deal of legendary matter, however, was mingled
with their information; and the account which passed in
the East, of the doctrines of the Pre-Socratic philosophers
can only be referred by us to the pseudepigraphs which

they consulted, or perhaps even to the opinions which had been developed in the East itself, and which they endeavoured to support with the authority of old Greek sages. But still, in every case, our thoughts must turn first of all to some Greek original.

11. It may be affirmed generally that the Syro-Arabs took up the thread of philosophy, precisely where the last of the Greeks had let it fall, that is, with the Neo-Platonic explanation of Aristotle, along with whose philosophy the works of Plato were also read and expounded. Among the Harranaeans, and for a long time in several Muslim sects, it was Platonic or Pythagorean-Platonic studies which were prosecuted with most ardour, — with which much that was Stoic or Neo-Platonic was associated. Extraordinary interest was taken in the fate of Socrates, who had suffered a martyr's death in heathen Athens for his rational belief. The Platonic teaching regarding the Soul and Nature exercised great influence. The Pythian utterance: "Know thyself", — handed down as the motto of the Socratic wisdom, and interpreted in a Neo-Platonic sense, — was ascribed by the Muslims to Ali, Mohammed's son-in-law, or even put into the mouth of the Prophet himself. "He who knows himself, knows God his Lord thereby": this was the text for Mystic speculations of all kinds.

In medical circles and at the worldly court, the works of Aristotle came more and more into favour, first of all of course the Logic and a few things from the Physical writings. The Logic — so they thought — was the only new thing the Stagyrite had discovered: in all the other sciences he agreed throughout with Pythagoras, Empedocles, Anaxagoras, Socrates and Plato. Accordingly Christian and Sabaean translators, and the circle influenced by them, drew their psychologico-ethical, political and metaphysical instruction without hesitation from the Pre-Aristotelian sages.

What bore the names of Empedocles, Pythagoras &c., was, naturally, spurious. Their wisdom is traced either to Hermes or to other wise men of the East. Thus Empedocles must have been a disciple of King David's, and afterwards of Loqman the Wise: Pythagoras must have sprung from the school of Solomon, — and so on. Writings which are cited in Arabic works as Socratic are, in so far as they are genuine, Platonic dialogues in which Socrates appears. Their quotations from Plato — not to speak of spurious writings — have a more or less comprehensive range: they are taken from the Apology, Krito, the Sophistes, Phaedrus, the Republic, Phaedo, Timäus and the Laws. That does not mean, however, that they possessed complete translations of all these works.

This much is certain, — that Aristotle did not reign as sole lord from the very outset. Plato, as they understood him, taught the Creation of the world, the Substantiality of the Spiritual, and the Immortality of the Soul. That teaching did no harm to the Faith. But Aristotle, with his doctrine of the Eternity of the World, and his less spiritualistic Psychology and Ethics, was regarded as dangerous. Muslim theologians of the 9th and 10th centuries, from various camps, wrote therefore against Aristotle. But circumstances altered. Philosophers arose by-and-by who rejected the Platonic doctrine of the One World-Soul, of which the souls of men are only transient parts, and sought grounds for their hope of immortality from Aristotle who attributed so great a significance to the Individual Substance.

12. The conception which was entertained of Aristotle in the period most remote, is best shown by the writings which were foisted upon him. Not only did they get his genuine works with Neo-Platonic interpretations attached to them, — not only was the treatise: "On the world" unhesitatingly acknowledged as Aristotelian, but he was also regarded as the author of many late-Greek productions, in which a Pythagorising Platonism or Neo-Platonism, or even a barren Syncretism was quite frankly taught.

Let us take here as our first example "the Book of the Apple" [1], wherein Aristotle plays the same part as Socrates in the Phaedo of Plato. As his end draws near, the Philosopher is visited by some of his disciples who find him in a cheerful frame of mind. This leads them to request their departing Master to give them some instruction about the Essence and Immortality of the Soul. Thereupon he discourses somewhat as follows: — "The Essence of the Soul consists in knowing, — in fact, in Philosophy, which is the highest form of knowing. A perfect knowledge of the truth constitutes therefore the blessedness which after death awaits the soul which is devoted to knowing. And just as knowing is rewarded with a higher knowledge, — so the punishment for not-knowing consists in a deeper ignorance. And really, there is nothing in Heaven or Earth, after all, except knowing and not-knowing, and the recompence which these two severally bring with them. Farther, — virtue is not essentially different from knowing; nor does vice differ

---

[1] The dialogue has received this name from the circumstance that during the conversation Aristotle holds in his hand an apple, the smell of which keeps awake what remains of his vital powers. At the close, his hand drops powerless, and the apple falls to the ground.

essentially from not-knowing. The relation of virtue to knowing, or of vice to not-knowing, is like that of water to ice: i. e. it is the same thing in a different form.

In knowing, — which is the divine essence of the Soul, — the Soul finds naturally its only true joy, and not in eating and drinking and sensual pleasure. For, sensual pleasure is a flame which merely warms for a short time; but the thinking Soul, — which longs for its deliverance from the murky world of the senses, — is a pure light that sheds a radiance far and wide. The Philosopher therefore is not afraid of death, but meets it gladly, when the Deity summons him. The enjoyment, which his limited knowledge affords him here is a guarantee to him of the rapture which the unveiling of the great world of the Unknown will procure him. Even already he knows something of this, for it is only through knowledge of the invisible, that the proper estimate of the sensible, on which he prides himself, is at all possible. He who comes to know his own self in this life, possesses in that very knowledge of himself the assurance of comprehending all things with an eternal knowledge, — i. e. of being immortal."

13. In the second place the so-called "Theology of Aristotle" may be referred to. In it Plato is represented as the Ideal-Man, who gains a knowledge of all things by means of an intuitive thinking, and thus has no need of the logical resources of Aristotle. Indeed, the highest reality — Absolute Being — is not apprehended by thinking, but only in an ecstatic Vision. "Often was I alone with my soul", says Aristotle-Plotinus, on this point. "Divested of the body, I entered as pure substance into my proper self, turning back from all that is external to what is

within. I was pure knowing there, at once the knowing
and the known. How astonished I was to behold beauty
and splendour in my proper self, and to recognize that I
was a part of the sublime Divine world, endowed even
with creative life! In this assurance of self, I was lifted
above the world of the senses, ay, even above the world
of spirits, up to the Divine state, where I beheld a light
so fair that no tongue can tell it, nor ear understand".

The soul forms the centre of the discussions in the
'Theology' also. All true human science is science of the
soul or knowledge of self, — knowledge of its essence, it is
true, coming first, and next in order, though less complete, knowledge of the operations of that essence. In
such knowledge, to which exceedingly few attain, the
highest wisdom consists, which does not admit of being
fully understood in the form of ideas, and which therefore
the philosopher like a skilful artist and wise lawgiver represents, for us men, in ever beautiful figures in religious
service. In this function precisely, the wise man comes forward as the potent, self-sufficing magician, whose knowledge lords it over the multitude, seeing that they remain
always bound in the fetters of outward things, of presentations and desires.

The soul stands in the centre of the All. Above it are
God and Intelligence, beneath it — Matter and Nature.
Its coming from God through Intelligence into Matter,
its presence in the body, its return on high — these are
the three *stadia* in which its life and that of the world
run their course. Matter and Nature, Sense-perception and
Presentation here lose their significance almost entirely. All
things exist by Intelligence (νοῦς, *'aql*). Intelligence con-

stitutes all things, and in Intelligence all things are One. The Soul too is Intelligence, but, so long as it stays in the body, it is Intelligence in hope, Intelligence in the form of longing. It longs for what is above, for the good and blessed stars, which spend their contemplative existence as sources of light, exalted above presentation and effort.

That then is the oriental Aristotle, as he was acknowledged by the earliest Peripatetics in Islam [1].

14. We need not wonder that the Easterns did not succeed in reaching an unadulterated conception of the Aristotelian philosophy. Our critical apparatus for discriminating between the genuine and the spurious was not in their possession. It must have proved even more difficult for them, to familiarize themselves with the world of Greek civilization, than for the Christian scholars of the Middle Ages, which had never entirely lost living touch with antiquity. In the East men remained dependent on Neo-Platonic redactions and interpretations. A part of the scientific system, to wit, the Politics of Aristotle, was a-wanting; and so, as a matter of course, the Laws or the Republic of Plato took its place. Only a few were aware of the difference between the two.

Another determining motive deserves notice. In their Neo-Platonic sources even, the Muslims came upon a harmonizing exposition of the Greek philosophers, and they felt constrained to adopt it. The first adherents of Aristotle were bound to assume a polemical and apologetic attitude. In opposition to, or in conformity with, the voice of the Muslim community, they required a coherent philosophy,

---

[1] Farther, an epitome of the στοιχείωσις θεολογική of Proclus, was held even in later times to be a genuine work of Aristotle's.

in which the One Truth must be found. The same rever-
ence, which Mohammed in his day had paid to the sacred
writings of the Jews and of the Christians, was shewn afterwards by Muslim scholars towards the works of Greek
philosophers; but these learned men exhibited greater fami-
liarity with their models, and less originality. In their eyes
the old philosophers were invested with an authority, to
which it was their duty to submit. The earliest Muslim
thinkers were so fully convinced of the superiority of Greek
knowledge that they did not doubt that it had attained
to the highest degree of certainty. The thought of making
farther and independent investigations did not readily occur
to an Oriental, who cannot imagine a man without a
teacher as being anything else than a disciple of Satan.
In accordance, therefore, with the precedent set by Hellenistic philosophers, an attempt had to be made to demonstrate the existence of the harmony between Plato and Aristotle, — and, in particular, to shelve tacitly those doctrines
which gave offence, or to exhibit them in a sense which
was not too decidedly contrary to Muslim Dogmatics. In
order to humour the opponents of Aristotle or of Philosophy in general, prominence was given to wise and edifying
sayings out of the philosopher's works, — both the genuine
and the spurious, — that so the way might be prepared
for the reception of his scientific thoughts. To the initiated,
however, the teaching of Aristotle, like that of other schools
and sects, was set forth as a higher truth, to which the
positive faith of the multitude and the more or less firmly
established system of the theologians were merely preliminary steps.

15. Muslim Philosophy has always continued to be an

Eclecticism which depended on their stock of works translated from the Greek. The course of its history has been a process of assimilation rather than of generation. It has not distinguished itself, either by propounding new problems or by any peculiarity in its endeavours to solve the old ones. It has therefore no important advances in thought to register. And yet, from a historical point of view, its significance is far greater than that of a mere intermediary between classical antiquity and Christian Scholasticism. To follow up the reception of Greek ideas into the mixed civilization of the East is a subject of historical interest possessing a charm entirely its own, especially if one can forget at the same time that once there were Greeks. But the consideration of this occurrence becomes important also by its presenting an opportunity for comparison with other civilizations. Philosophy is a phenomenon so unique — so thoroughly indigenous and independent a growth of Grecian soil — that one might regard it as being exempt from the conditions of general civilized life, and as being explicable only *per se*. Now the History of Philosophy in Islam is valuable, just because it sets forth the first attempt to appropriate the results of Greek thinking, with greater comprehensiveness and freedom than in the early Christian dogmatics. Acquaintance with the conditions which made such an attempt possible, will permit us to reach conclusions, by way of analogical reasonings — though with precaution, and for the present at least, to a very limited extent — as to the reception of Graeco-Arab science in the Christian Middle Ages, and will perhaps teach us a little about the conditions under which Philosophy arises in general.

We can hardly speak of a Muslim philosophy in the

proper sense of the term. But there were many men in Islam who could not keep from philosophizing; and even through the folds of the Greek drapery, the form of their own limbs is indicated. It is easy to look down on these men, from the high watch-tower of some School-Philosophy, but it will be better for us to get to know them and to comprehend them in their historical environment. We must leave to special research the tracing of each thought up to its origin. Our aim in what follows can be nothing more than to point out what the Muslims constructed out of the materials which were before them.

II. PHILOSOPHY AND ARAB KNOWLEDGE.

1. Grammatical Science.

By Muslim scholars of the 10th century the sciences were divided into 'Arab Sciences' and 'Old'- or 'Non-Arab Sciences'. To the former belonged Grammar, Ethics and Dogmatics, History and Knowledge of Literature; to the latter Philosophy, Natural Science and Medicine. In the main the division is a proper one. The last-named branches are not only those which were determined the most by foreign influences, but those too which never became really popular. And yet the so called 'Arab Sciences' are not altogether pure native products. They too arose or were developed in places in the Muslim empire where Arabs and Non-Arabs met together, and where the need was awakened of reflecting on those subjects which concern mankind the most, — Speech and Poetry, Law and Religion, — in so far as differences or inadequacies appeared therein. In the mode in which this came about, it is easy to trace the influence of Non-Arabs, particularly of Persians; and the part taken by Greek Philosophy in the process asserts itself in ever-growing importance.

2. The Arabic language, — in which the Arabs themselves took particular delight, for its copious vocabulary,

its wealth of forms and its inherent capability of cultivation, — was peculiarly fitted to take a leading position
in the world. If it is compared, for example, with the un-
wieldy Latin, or even with the turgid Persian, it is found
to be specially distinguished by the possession of short
Abstract-forms, — a property of great service in scientific
expression. It is capable of indicating the finest shades of
meaning; but just because of its richly developed stock of
synonyms, it offers temptations to deviate from the Aristotelian rule, — that the use of synonyms is not permis-
sible in exact science. A language so elegant, expressive,
and difficult withal, as Arabic was, necessarily invited much
examination, when it had become the polite language of
the Syrians and the Persians. Above all, the study of the
Koran, and the recital and interpretation of it demanded
profound attention to be devoted to the language. Un-
believers, also, may have thought that they could point
out grammatical errors in the sacred Book; and therefore
examples were gathered out of ancient poems and out of
the living speech of the Bedouins, to support the expressions of the Koran. To these examples remarks were, no
doubt, added upon grammatical accuracy in general. On
the whole, the living usage formed the standard, but in
order to save the authority of the Koran, it was certainly
not applied without artifice. This proceeding was regarded,
all the same, by simple believers, with a measure of sus-
picion. Masudi tells us even of some grammarians from
Basra, who, when on a pleasure trip, took to going through
a Koran Imperative, and for that reason (?) were soundly
cudgelled by country folk engaged in date-gathering.

3. The Arabs trace their grammatical science, like so

many other things, to Ali, to whom is ascribed even Aristotle's tripartite division of speech. In reality the study began to be cultivated in Basra and Kufa. Its earliest development is involved in obscurity, for in the Grammar of Sibawaih († 786) we have a finished system, — a colossal work —, which, like Ibn Sina's Canon of Medicine in after times, could only be explained by later generations as the production of many scholars working in collaboration. We are but ill-informed even on the points of difference between the schools of Basra and Kufa. The Basra grammarians, like the school of Bagdad in subsequent times, must have conceded a great influence to *Qiyas* (Analogy) in the determination of grammatical phenomena, while those of Kufa allowed many idiomatic forms which diverged from Qiyas. On this ground, to mark the contrast between the Basra grammarians and those of Kufa, the former were called 'the Logic people'. Their terminology differed in detail from that of the Kufa school. Many, whose heads had been turned by logic, in the opinion of the genuine Arabs, must have gone decidedly too far in their captious criticism of the language; but on the other side caprice was raised to the position of rule.

It was from no mere accident that the school of Basra was the first to avail itself of logical resources. Generally speaking, it was at Basra that the influence of philosophic doctrines first appeared, and among its grammarians were to be found many Shi'ites and Mutazilites, who readily permitted foreign wisdom to influence their doctrinal teaching.

4. Grammatical science, in so far as it was not confined, to the collecting of Examples, Synonyms &c., when so determined by the subjects specially treated, was affected

by the Aristotelian Logic. Even before the Muslim era, Syrians and Persians had studied the treatise περὶ ἑρμηνείας, with Stoic and Neo-Platonic additions. Ibn al-Moqaffa, who at first was intimate with the grammarian Khalil (v. *infra*), then made accessible to the Arabs all that existed in Pahlawi of a grammatical or logical nature. In conformity therewith the various kinds of Sentences were enumerated, — at one time five, at another eight or nine, as well as the three parts of speech, — Noun, Verb and Particle. Afterwards some scholars, like Djahiz, included syllogistic figures among the Rhetorical figures; and in later representations there was much disputation about Sound and Idea. The question was discussed whether language is the result of ordinance or a product of nature; but gradually the philosophic view preponderated, that it came by ordinance.

Next to Logic the influence of the preparatory or mathematical sciences falls to be noticed here. Like the prose of ordinary intercourse and the rhymes of the Koran, the verses of the poets were not only collected but also arranged according to special principles of classification, — for example, according to metre. After Grammar Prosody arose. Khalil († 791), the teacher of Sibawaih, to whom the first application of Qiyas to grammatical science was attributed, is said even to have created metrical science. While language came to be regarded as the national, conventional element in poetry, the notion was entertained that what was natural, and common to all populations, would be found in their metre. Thabit ibn Qorra (836—901) therefore maintained, in his classification of the sciences, that metre was something essential, and the study of metre a natural science, and therefore a branch of philosophy.

5. Grammatical science, nevertheless, limited as it was to the Arabic language, retained its peculiarities, upon which this is not the place to enter. At all events, it is an imposing production of the keenly-observing and diligently-collecting Arab intelligence, — a production of which the Arabs might well be proud. An apologist of the 10th century, who was engaged in combating Greek philosophy, said: "He who is acquainted with the subtleties and profundities of Arab poetry and versification, knows well that they surpass all such things as numbers, lines and points, which are wont to be advanced in proof of their opinions, by people who idly dream that they are capable of understanding the essence of things. I cannot see the substantial advantage of things like numbers, lines and points, if, in spite of the trifling profit which may attend them, they do harm to the Faith and are followed by consequences, against which we have to invoke the help of God." Men would not have their delight in the minutiae of their language disturbed by general philosophic speculations. Many a word-form, originating with the translators of foreign works, was held in detestation by purist Grammarians. The beautiful art of caligraphy, more decorative in its nature than constructive, like Arabic art in general, became developed in noble, delicate forms, and met with a wider expansion than scientific research into the language. In the very characters of the Arabic speech, we may still see the subtlety of the intelligence which formed them, although at the same time we may see a lack of energy, which is observable in the entire development of Arab culture.

2. ETHICAL TEACHING.

1. The believing Muslim, in so far as custom did not maintain its dominion over him, had at first the Word of God and the example of His Prophet as his rule of conduct and opinion. After the Prophet's death, the Sunna of Mohammed was followed, in cases where the Koran gave no information, — that is to say, men acted and decided, as Mohammed had decided or acted, according to the Tradition of his Companions. But from the time of the conquest of countries in possession of an old civilization, demands which were altogether new were made of Islam. Instead of the simple conditions of Arab life, usages and institutions were met with there, in regard to which the Sacred Law gave no precise direction, and to meet which no tradition or interpretation of tradition presented itself. Every day added thus to the number of individual cases which had not been provided for, and yet about which one had to come to a decision, whether according to custom, or his own sense of right. In the old-Roman provinces, Syria and Mesopotamia, Roman law must have long continued to exercise an important influence.

Those jurists who attributed to their own opinion (*Ra'y, opinio*) alongside of the Koran and Sunna, a subsidiary authority to determine the law, were called 'Adherents of the Ra'y'. One of them, Abu Hanifa of Kufa († 767), the founder of the Hanifite School, became specially famous. But even in Medina, before the appearance of the school of Malik (715—795), as well as in that school, a harmless though restricted deference was at first paid to the Ra'y. By slow degrees, however, and in the course of opposing a Ra'y which was becoming a pretext for much arbitrariness, the view gained ground, that in everything the Tradition (*hadith*) respecting the Sunna of the Prophet was to be followed. Thereupon traditions were collected from all quarters, and explained — and in large numbers even forged —; and a system of criteria to determine their genuineness was formed, which, however, laid more stress upon the external evidence and the appropriateness of the traditionary material than upon consistency and historic truth. As a consequence of this development, the 'people of the Ra'y', who were chiefly located in Iraq (Babylonia), were now confronted by the 'Adherents of the Tradition', or the Medina school. Even Shafii (767—820), the founder of the third school of Law, who in general held to the Sunna, was numbered with the partisans of Tradition, in contradistinction no doubt to Abu Hanifa.

2. Logic introduced a new element into this controversy, — viz *Qiyas* or Analogy. There had been, of course, stray applications of Qiyas, even in earlier times; but, to lay down Qiyas as a principle, a foundation or a source of law, — presupposed the influence of scientific reflection. Although the terms *Ra'y* and *Qiyas* may be used as synonyms, yet there is in the latter term, less suggestion of the presence and operation of individual predilection than there is in *Ra'y*. The more one grew accustomed to employ Qiyas in grammatical and logical researches, the more readily could he include this principle in the institutes of jurisprudence, whether by way of reasoning from one instance to another, or from the majority of instances to the remainder (i. e. analogically), or by way of seeking rather for some common ground governing various cases,

from which the conduct proper in a particular case might be deduced (i. e. syllogistically)[1].

The application of Qiyas appears to have come into use, first and most extensively, in the Hanifite school, but afterwards also in the school of Shafii, — though with a more limited range. In connection therewith, the question — whether language was capable of expressing the Universal, or could merely denote the Particular — became important for ethical doctrine.

The logical principle of Qiyas never attained to great repute. Much more emphasis was laid, — next to the Koran and the Sunna, the historic foundations of the Law —, upon the *Idjma*, that is, the Consensus of the Congregation of the faithful. The Consensus of the Congregation or, practically, of the most influential learned men in it, — who may be compared to the fathers and teachers of the Catholic Church, — is the Dogmatical principle, which, contested only by a few, has proved the most important instrument in establishing the Muslim Ethical System. Theory, however, continues to assign a certain subordinate place to Qiyas, as a fourth source of moral guidance, after Koran, Sunna and Idjma.

3. The Muslim Ethical System (*al-fiqh*) = 'the knowledge') takes into account the entire life of the believer, for whom the Faith itself is the first of all duties. Like every innovation the system at first encountered violent opposition: — commandment was now turned into doctrinal theory, and

---

[1] Examples of both methods occur, but usually *Qiyas* is equivalent to *Analogy*. However, in the philosophical terminology which owes its origin to the Translators, *Qiyas* always stands for συλλογισμός, while ἀναλογία is rendered by the Arabic *mithl*.

believing obedience into abstruse pursuit of knowledge: that called for protestation alike from plain pious people and from wise statesmen. But gradually the 'knowing' men or men learned in the Law (*ulamā*, or in the West, *faqihs*) were recognized as the true heirs of the prophets. The Ethical system was developed before the Doctrinal, and it has been able to hold the leading position up to the present day. Nearly every Muslim knows something of it, seeing it is part of a good religious upbringing. According to the great Church-father Gazali, 'the Fiqh' is the daily bread of believing souls, while the Doctrine is only valuable as a Medicine for the sick.

We are not called upon here to enter into the minutiae of the fine-spun casuistic of the Fiqh. The main subject handled in it is an ideal righteousness, which can never be illustrated in all its purity in our imperfect world. We are acquainted now with its principles, and with the position which it holds in Islam. Let us merely add a brief notice of the division of moral acts which was formulated by ethical teachers. According to this classification there are:

1. Acts, the practice of which is an absolute duty and is therefore rewarded, and the omission of which is punished:

2. Acts which are recommended by the Law, and are the subject of reward, but the neglect of which does not call for punishment:

3. Acts which are permitted, but which in the eyes of the Law are a matter of indifference:

4. Acts which the Law disapproves of, but does not hold as punishable:

5. Acts which are forbidden by the Law and which demand unconditional punishment [1].

4. Greek philosophic enquiries have had a two-fold influence upon the Ethics of Islam. With many of the sectaries and mystics, both orthodox and heretic, an ascetic system of Ethics is found, coloured by Pythagorean-Platonic views. The same thing appears with philosophers, whom we shall afterwards meet again. But in orthodox circles the Aristotelian deliverance, — that virtue consists in the just mean —, found much acceptance, because something similar stood in the Koran, and because, generally, the tendency of Islam was a catholic one, — one conciliatory of opposites.

More attention indeed was given to Politics than to Ethics, in the Muslim empire, and the struggles of political parties were the first thing to occasion difference of opinion. Disputes about the *Imâmat*, i. e. the headship in the Muslim Church, pervade the entire history of Islam ; but the questions discussed have commonly more of a personal and practical than a theoretical importance, and therefore a history of philosophy does not need to consider them very fully. Hardly anything of philosophic value emerges in them. Even in the course of the first centuries there was developed a firm body of constitutional law canonically expressed; but this, like the ideal system of duty, was not particularly heeded by strong rulers, — who viewed it as mere theological brooding, — while, on the other hand, by weak princes it could not be applied at all.

Just as little is it worth our while to examine minutely the numerous 'mirrors of Princes', which were such favou-

---

[1] Cf. Snouck Hurgronje in ZDMG, LIII p. 155.

rites, in Persia especially, and in whose wise moral saws, and maxims of political sagacity, the courtly circles found edification.

The weight of philosophic endeavour in Islam lies on the theoretical and intellectual side. With the actual proceedings of social and political life they are able to make but a scanty compromise. Even the Art of the Muslims, although it exhibits more originality than their Science, does not know how to animate the crude material, but merely sports with ornamental forms. Their Poetry creates no Drama, and their Philosophy is unpractical.

3. DOCTRINAL SYSTEMS.

1. In the Koran there had been given to Muslims a religion, but no system, — precepts but no doctrines. What is contrary to logic therein, — what we account for by the shifting circumstances of the Prophet's life, and his varying moods, — was simply accepted by the first believers, without asking questions about the How and Why. But in the conquered countries they were faced by a fully-formed Christian Dogmatic as well as by Zoroastrian and Brahmanic theories. We have laid frequent stress already upon the great debt which the Muslims owe to the Christians; and the doctrinal system has certainly been determined the most by Christian influences. In Damascus the formation of Muslim Dogmas was affected by Orthodox and Monophysite teaching, and in Basra and Bagdad rather perhaps by Nestorian and Gnostic theories. Little of the literature belonging to the earliest period of this movement has come down to us, but we cannot be

wrong in assigning a considerable influence to personal intercourse and regular school-instruction. Not much was learned in the East at that time out of books, any more than it is to-day: more was learned from the lips of the teacher. The similarity between the oldest doctrinal teachings in Islam and the dogmas of Christianity is too great to permit any one to deny that they are directly connected. In particular, the first question about which there was much dispute, among Muslim Scholars, was that of the Freedom of the Will. Now the freedom of the will was almost universally accepted by Oriental Christians. At no time and in no place perhaps was the Will-problem — first in the Christology, but afterward in the Anthropology — so much discussed from every point as in the Christian circles of the East at the time of the Muslim conquest.

Besides these considerations which are partly of an *a priori* character, there are also detached notices which indicate that some of the earliest Muslims, who taught the Freedom of the Will, had Christian teachers.

A number of purely philosophic elements from the Gnostic systems, and afterwards from the translation-literature, associated themselves with the Hellenistic-Christian influences.

2. An assertion, expressed in logical or dialectic fashion, whether verbal or written, was called by the Arabs, — generally, but more particularly in religious teaching — a *Kalam* (λόγος), and those who advanced such assertions were called *Mutakallimun*. The name was transferred from the individual assertion to the entire system, and it covered also the introductory, elementary observations on Method,

— and so on. Our best designation for the science of the Kalam is 'Theological Dialectics' or simply 'Dialectics'; and in what follows we may translate *Mutakallimun* by 'Dialecticians'.

The name *Mutakallimun*, which was at first common to all the Dialecticians, was in later times applied specially to the Antimutazilite and Orthodox theologians. In the latter case it might be well, following the sense, to render the term by Dogmatists or Schoolmen. In fact while the first dialecticians had the Dogma still to form, those who came later had only to expound and establish it.

The introduction of Dialectics into Islam was a violent innovation, and it was vehemently denounced by the party of the Tradition. Whatever went beyond the regular ethical teaching was heresy to them, for faith should be obedience, and not, — as was maintained by the Murdjites and Mutazilites —, knowledge. By the latter it was laid down without reserve that speculation was one of the duties of believers. Even to this demand the times became reconciled, for according to tradition the Prophet had said already: 'The first thing which God created was Knowledge or Reason'.

3. Very numerous are the various opinions which found utterance in the days even of the Omayyads, but especially in those of the early Abbasids. The farther they diverged from one another, the more difficult it was for the men of the Tradition to come to an understanding with them; but gradually certain compact doctrinal collections stood out distinctly, of which the rationalist system of the Mutazilites, the successors of the Qadarites, was most widely extended, particularly among Shi'ites. From Caliph Mamun's

time down to Mutawakkil's, it even received State recognition; and the Mutazilites, who had been in earlier days oppressed and persecuted by the temporal power, now became Inquisitors of the Faith themselves, with whom the sword supplied the place of argument. About the same time, however, their opponents the Traditionalists commenced to build up a system of belief. Upon the whole there was no lack of intermediary forms between the naive Faith of the multitude and the Gnosis of the dialecticians. In contrast to the spiritualistic stamp of Mutazilitism these intermediary forms took an anthropomorphic character with regard to the doctrine of the Deity, and a materialistic character with regard to the theory of man and the universe (Anthropology and Cosmology). The soul, for example, was conceived of by them as corporeal, or as an accident of the body, and the Divine Essence was imagined as a human body. The religious teaching and art of the Muslims were greatly averse to the symbolical God-Father of the Christians, but there was an abundance of absurd speculations about the form of Allah. Some went so far as to ascribe to him all the bodily members together, with the exception of the beard and other privileges of oriental manhood.

It is impossible to discuss in detail all the Dialectic sects, which often made their first appearance in the form of political parties. From the standpoint of the history of Philosophy it is enough to give here the chief doctrines of the Mutazilites, in so far as they can lay claim to general interest.

4. The first question, then, concerned man's conduct and destiny. The forerunners of the Mutazilites, who were

called Qadarites, taught the Freedom of the human Will; and the Mutazilites, even in later times, when their speculations were directed more to theologico-metaphysical problems, were first and foremost pointed to as the supporters of the doctrine of Divine Righteousness, — which gives rise to no evil, and rewards or punishes man according to his deserts —, and, in the second place, as the confessors, or avowed supporters of the Unity of God, i. e. the absence of properties from his Essence considered *per se* [or the predicateless character of the essential nature of God]. The systematic statement of their doctrines must have been influenced by the Logicians (v. 1V, 2 § 1); for even in the first half of the 10th century, the Mutazilite system began with the confession of the Unity of God, while the doctrine of God's Righteousness, announced as it is in all his works, is relegated to the second place.

The responsibility of man, as well as the holiness of God, who is incapable of directly causing man's sinful actions, had to be saved by asserting the freedom of the Will. Man must therefore be lord of his actions; but he is lord of these only, for few entertained any doubt that the energy which confers ability to act at all, and the power of doing either a good or a bad action come to man from God. Hence the numerous subtle discussions, — amalgamated with a criticism of the philosophic con-ception of Time — on the question whether the power, which God creates in man, is bestowed previous to the action, or coincidently and simultaneously therewith: For, did the power precede the act, then it would either have to last up to the time of the act, which would belie its accidental character (cf. II, 3 § 12), or have ceased to exist before the act, — in which case it might have been dispensed with altogether.

From human conduct speculation passed on to consider the operations of nature. Instead of God and man, the antithesis in this case is God and nature. The productive and generative powers of nature were recognized as means or proximate causes; and some endeavoured to investigate them. In their opinion, however, nature herself, like all the world, was a work of God, a creature of his wisdom: And just as the omnipotence of God was limited in the moral kingdom by his holiness or righteousness, — so in the natural world it was limited by his wisdom. Even the presence of evil and mischief in the world was accounted for by the wisdom of God, who sends everything for the best. A production or object of Divine activity, evil is not. "God may be able, indeed," — so an earlier generation had maintained — "to act wickedly and unreasonably, but he would not do it." The later Mutazilites taught, on the other hand, that God has no power at all to do anything which is in this way repugnant to his nature. Their opponents, who regarded God's unlimited might and unfathomable will as directly operative in all doing and effecting were indignant at this teaching, and compared its propounders to the dualistic Magians. Consistent Monism was on the side of these opponents, who did not care to turn man and nature into creators — next to and under God — of their acts or operations.

5. The Mutazilites, it is clear from the foregoing, had a different idea of God from that which was entertained by the multitude and by the Traditionalists. This became specially evident, as speculation advanced, in the doctrine

of the Divine attributes. From the very beginning the Unity of God was strongly emphasized in Islam; but that did not prevent men from bestowing upon him many beautiful names following human analogy, and ascribing to him several attributes. Of these the following came gradually into greatest prominence, under the influence assuredly of Christian dogmatics: — viz.: Wisdom, Power, Life, Will, Speech or Word, Sight and Hearing. The last two of these — Sight and Hearing — were the first to be explained in a spiritual sense, or entirely set aside. But the absolute Unity of the Godhead did not appear to be compatible with any plurality of co-eternal attributes. Would not that be the Trinity of the Christians, who before now had explained the three Persons of the One Divine Being as attributes? In order to avoid this inconvenience they sought sometimes to derive several attributes out of others by a process of abstraction, and to refer them to a single one — for instance to Knowledge or Power — and sometimes to apprehend them each and all as being states of the Divine essence, or to identify them with the essence itself, in which case of course their significance nearly disappeared. Occasionally an attempt was made through refinements of phraseology to save something of that significance. While, for example, a philosopher, denying the attributes, maintained that God is by his essence a Being who knows, a Mutazilite dialectian expressed it thus: God is a Being who knows, but by means of a knowledge, which He himself is.

In the opinion of the Traditionalists the conception of God was in this way being robbed of all its contents. The Mutazilites hardly got beyond negative determinations,

— that God is not like the things of this world, — that
he is exalted above Space, Time, Movement, and so on;
but they held fast to the doctrine that he is the Creator
of the world. Although little could be asserted regarding
the Being of God, it was thought he could be known
from his works.

For the Mutazilites as well as for their opponents, the
Creation was an absolute act of God, and the existence of
the world an existence in time. They energetically combated the doctrine of the eternity of the world, — a
doctrine supported by the Aristotelian philosophy, and
which had been widely spread throughout the East.

6. We have already found 'Speech' or 'the Word', given
as one of the eternal attributes of God; and, probably by
way of conformity with the Christian doctrine of the
Logos, there was taught in particular the eternity of the
Koran which had been revealed to the Prophet. This belief
in an eternal Koran by the side of Allah, was downright
idolatry, according to the Mutazilites; and in opposition
thereto the Mutazilite Caliphs proclaimed it as a doctrine
accepted by the State, — that the Koran had been created:
Whoever denied this doctrine was publicly punished. Now
although the Mutazilites in maintaining this dogma were
more in harmony with the original Islam than their opponents, yet history has justified the latter, for pious needs
proved stronger than logical conclusions. Many of the Mutazilites, in the opinion of their brethren in the faith, were
far too ready to make light of the Koran, the Word of God.
If it did not agree with their theories, it received ever new
interpretations. In actual fact reason had more weight with
many than the revealed Book. By comparing not only the

three revealed religions together, but these also with Persian and Indian religious teaching and with philosophic speculation, they reached a natural religion, which reconciled opposites. This was built up on the basis of an inborn knowledge, universally necessary, — that there is one God, who, as a wise Creator, has produced the world, and also endowed Man with reason that he may know his Creator and distinguish between Good and Evil. Contrasted with this Natural or Rational religion, acquaintance with the teaching of revelation is then something adventitious, — an acquired knowledge.

By this contention the most consistent of the Mutazilites had broken away from the consensus of the Muslim religious community, and had thus actually put themselves outside the general faith. At first they still appealed to that consensus, — which they were able to do as long as the secular power was favourably disposed to them. That condition, however, did not last long, and they soon learned by experience what has often been taught since, — that the communities of men are more ready to accept a religion sent down to them from on high, than an enlightened explanation of it.

7. Following up this survey let us take a closer view of one or two of the most considerable of the Mutazilites, that the general picture may not be wanting in individual features.

Let us first glance at Abu-l-Hudhail al-Allaf, who died about the middle of the 9th century. He was a famous dialectician, and one of the first who allowed philosophy to exercise an influence on their theological doctrines.

That an attribute should be capable of inhering in a

Being in any way is not conceivable, in the opinion of
Abu-l-Hudhail: It must either be identical with the Being
or different from it. But yet he looks about for some way
of adjustment. God is, according to him, knowing, mighty,
living, through knowledge, might and life, which are his
very essence; and just as men had done even before this,
on the Christian side, he terms these three predicates the
Modi (*wudjuh*) of the Divine Being. He agrees also that
hearing, seeing and other attributes are eternal in God,
but only with regard to the world which was afterwards
to be created. Besides, it would be easy enough for him
and for others, who were affected by the philosophy of the
day, to interpret these and similar expressions — such as
God's 'beholding' on the last day, [1] — in a spiritual sense,
since generally they regarded seeing and hearing as spiritual
acts. For example, Abu-l-Hudhail maintained that motion
was visible, but not palpable, because it was not a body.

The Will of God, however, is not to be regarded as
eternal. On the contrary, Abu-l-Hudhail assumes absolute
declarations of Will as being different both from the Being
who wills and the object which is willed. Thus the absolute
Word of Creation takes an intermediate position between
the eternal Creator and the transient created world. These
declarations of God's Will form a kind of intermediate essence,
to be compared with the Platonic Ideas or the Sphere-spirits,
but perhaps regarded rather as immaterial powers than as
personal spirits. Abu-l-Hudhail distinguishes between the
absolute Word of Creation and the accidental Word of Revelation, which is announced to men in the form of command
and prohibition, appearing as matter and in space, and which

---

[1] For this the Mystics introduced a sixth sense.

is thus significant only for this transient world. The possibility of living in accordance with the Divine word of revelation, or of resisting it, exists therefore in this life alone. Binding injunction and prohibition presuppose Freedom of Will and capability of acting in accordance therewith. On the other hand in the future life there are no obligations in the form of laws, and, accordingly, no longer any freedom : everything there depends on the absolute determination of God. Nor will there be any motion in the world beyond, for as motion has once had a beginning, it must, at the end of the world, come to a close in everlasting rest. Abu-l-Hudhail, therefore, could not have believed in a resurrection of the body.

Human actions he divides into Natural and Moral, or Actions of the members, and Actions of the heart. An action is moral, only when we perform it without constraint. The moral act is Man's own property, acquired by his own exertions, but his knowledge comes to him from God, partly through Revelation, and partly through the light of Nature.

Anterior even to any revelation man is instructed in duty by Nature, and thus is fully enabled to know God, to discern Good from Evil, and to live a virtuous, honest and upright life.

8. Noteworthy as a man and a thinker is a younger contemporary of Abu-l-Hudhail's, and apparently a disciple of his, commonly called Al-Nazzam, who died in the year 845. A fanciful, restless, ambitious man, not a consistent thinker, but yet a bold and honest one, — such is the representation of him given us by Djahiz, one of his pupils. The people considered him a madman or a heretic. A good deal in his teaching is in touch with what passed among

the Orientals as the Philosophy of Empedocles and Anaxagoras
(Cf. also Abu-l-Hudhail).

In the opinion of Nazzam God can do absolutely no
evil thing; in fact he can only do that which he knows
to be the best thing for his servants. His omnipotence
reaches no farther than what he actually does. Who could
hinder him from giving effect to the splendid exuberance
of his Being? A Will, in the proper sense of the term,
— which invariably implies a need, — is by no means to
be attributed to God. The Will of God, on the contrary,
is only a designation of the Divine agency itself, or of the
commands which have been conveyed to men. Creation is
an act performed once for all, in which all things were
made at one and the same time, so that one thing is
contained in another, and so that in process of time the various
specimens of minerals, plants and animals, as well as the
numerous children of Adam, gradually emerge from their
latent condition and come to the light.

Nazzam, like the philosophers, rejects the theory of atoms
(v. II, 3 § 12), but then he can only account for the traversing of a definite distance, by reason of the infinite
divisibility of space, by postulating leaps. He holds bodily
substances to be composed of 'accidents' instead of atoms.
And just as Abu-l-Hudhail could not conceive of the in-
herence of attributes in an essence, so Nazzam can only
imagine the accident as the substance itself or as a part
of the substance. Thus 'Fire' or 'the Warm', for instance,
exists in a latent condition in wood, but it becomes free
when, by means of friction, its antagonist 'the Cold' disappears. In the process there occurs a motion or transposition,
but no qualitative change. Sensible qualities, such as

colours, savours and odours, are, in Nazzam's view, bodies.

Even the soul or the intellect of Man he conceives to be a finer kind of body. The soul, of course, is the most excellent part of man: it completely pervades the body, which is its organ, and it must be termed the real and true Man. Thoughts and aspirations are defined as Movements of the Soul.

In matters of Faith and in questions of Law Nazzam rejects both the consensus of the congregation and the analogical interpretation of the Law, and appeals in Shi'ite fashion to the infallible Imam. He thinks it possible for the whole body of Muslims to concur in admitting an erroneous doctrine, as, for instance, the doctrine that Mohammed has a mission for all mankind in contradistinction to other prophets. Whereas God sends every prophet to all mankind.

Nazzam, besides, shares the view of Abu-l-Hudhail as to the knowledge of God and of moral duties by means of the reason. He is not particularly convinced of the inimitable excellence of the Koran. The abiding marvel of the Koran is made to consist only in the fact that Mohammed's contemporaries were kept from producing something like to the Koran.

He has certainly not retained much of the Muslim Eschatology. At least the torments of hell are in his view resolved into a process of consuming by fire.

9. Many syncretistic doctrines, but all devoid of originality, have come down to us from the school of Nazzam. The most famous man, whom it produced was the elegant writer and Natural-Philosopher Djahiz († 860), who demanded of the genuine scholar that he should combine the study

of Theology with that of Natural Science. He traces in all things the operations of Nature, but also a reference in these operations to the Creator of the world. Man's reason is capable of knowing the Creator, and in like manner of comprehending the need of a prophetic revelation. Man's only merit is in his will, for on the one hand all his actions are interwoven with the events of Nature, and on the other his entire knowledge is necessarily determined from above. And yet no great significance appears to accrue to the Will, which is derived from 'knowing'. At least Will in the Divine Being is quite negatively conceived of, that is, God never operates unconsciously, or with dislike to his work.

In all this there is little that is original. His ethical ideal is 'the mean', and the style of his genius is also mediocre. It is only in compiling his numerous writings that Djahiz has shown any excess.

10. With the earlier Mutazilites reflections on Ethics and Natural Philosophy predominate; with those who come later Logico-metaphysical meditations prevail. In particular Neo-Platonic influences are to be traced here.

Muammar, whose date cannot be accurately determined, although it may be set down as about the year 900, has much in common with those who have just been named. But he is far more emphatic in his denial of the existence of Divine attributes, which he regards as being contradictory of the absolute unity of the Divine essence. God is high above every form of plurality. He knows neither himself nor any other being, for 'knowing' would presuppose a plurality in him. He is even to be called Hyper-eternal. Nevertheless he is to be recognized as Creator of the world. He has only created bodies, it is true; and these of themselves

create their Accidents, whether through operation of Nature
or by Will. The number of these accidents is infinite, for
in their essence they are nothing more than the intellectual
relations of thought. Muammar is a Conceptualist. Motion
and Rest, Likeness and Unlikeness, and so on, are nothing
in themselves, and have merely an intellectual or ideal
existence. The soul, which is held to be the true essence of
Man, is conceived of as an Idea or an immaterial substance,
though it is not clearly stated how it is related to the
body or to the Divine essence. The account handed down
is confused.

Man's will is free, and, — properly speaking, — Willing
is his only act, for the outward action belongs to the body
(Cf. Djahiz).

The school of Bagdad, to which Muammar seems to
belong, was conceptualist. With the exception of the most
general predicates, — those of Being and Becoming, it
made Universals subsist only as notions or concepts. Abu
Hashim of Basra († 933) stood nearer to Realism. The attributes of God, as well as Accidents and Genus-notions in
general, were regarded by him as something in a middle
position between Being and Not-Being: he called them
Conditions or Modes. He designated Doubt as a requisite
in all knowing. A simple Realist he was not.

Mutazilite thinkers indulged in dialectic quibbling even
about 'Not-Being'. They argued that Not-Being, as well
as Being, must come to possess a kind of reality, seeing
that it may become the subject of thought: at least man
tries to think of 'Nothing' rather than not think at all.

11. In the 9th century several dialectic systems had been
formed in the contest against the Mutazilites, one of which,

viz. the Karramite system, held its ground till long after the 10th century. There arose, however, from the ranks of the Mutazilites a man whose mission it was to reconcile antagonistic views, and who set up that doctrinal system which was acknowledged as orthodox first in the East, and, later, throughout the whole of Islam. This was Al-Ashari (873—935), who understood how to render to God the things that are God's, and to man the things that are man's. He rejected the rude anthropomorphism of the Antimutazilite dialecticians, and set God high above all that is bodily and human, while he left to the Deity his omnipotence, and his universal agency. With him Nature lost all her efficaciousness; but for man a certain distinction was reserved, consisting in his being able to give assent to the works which were accomplished in him by God, and to claim these as his own. Nor was Man's sensuous-spiritual being interfered with: He was permitted to hope for the resurrection of the body and the beholding of God. As regards the Koranic revelation, Ashari distinguished between an eternal Word in God, and the Book as we possess it, which latter was revealed in Time.

In the detailed statement of his doctrines Ashari showed no originality in any way, but merely arranged and condensed the material given him, — a proceeding which could not be carried out without discrepancies. The main thing, however, was that his Cosmology, Anthropology and Eschatology did not depart too far from the text of the Tradition for the edification of pious souls, and that his theology, in consequence of a somewhat spiritualized conception of God was not altogether unsatisfactory even to men of higher culture.

Ashari relies upon the revelation contained in the Koran. He does not recognize any rational knowledge with regard to Divine things that is independent of the Koran. The senses are not in general likely to deceive us, but on the other hand our judgment may easily do so. We know God, it is true, by our reason, but only from Revelation, which is the one source of such knowledge.

According to Ashari, then, God is first of all the omnipotent Creator. Farther he is omniscient: he knows what men do and what they wish to do: he knows also what happens, and how that which does not happen would have happened, if it had happened. Moreover all predicates which express any perfection are applicable to God, with the proviso that they apply to him in another and higher sense than to his creatures. In creating and sustaining the world God is the sole cause: all worldly events proceed continually and directly from him. Man, however, is quite conscious of the difference between his involuntary movements, such as shivering and shaking, and those which are carried out in the exercise of his will and choice.

12. The most characteristic theory which the dialectic of the Muslims has fashioned, is their doctrine of Atoms. The development of this doctrine is still wrapped in great obscurity. It was advocated by the Mutazilites but particularly by their opponents before the time of Ashari. Our sketch shows how it was held in the Asharite school, where partly perhaps it was first developed.

The Atomic doctrine of the Muslim dialecticians had its source, of course, in Greek Natural Philosophy; but its reception and farther development were determined by the requirements of theological Polemic and Apologetic. The

like phenomenon may be observed in the case of individual
Jews and among believing Catholics. It is impossible to
suppose that Atomism was taken up in Islam, merely because Aristotle had fought against it. Here we have to
register a desperate struggle for a religious advantage, and
one in which weapons are not chosen at will: It is the
end that decides. Nature has to be explained, not from
herself but from some divine creative act; and this world
must be regarded not as an eternal and divine order of
things, but as a creature of transient existence. God must
be thought of and spoken of as a freely-working and almighty Creator, not as an impersonal cause or inactive
primeval source. Accordingly, from the earliest times the
doctrine of the creation is placed at the apex of Muslim
dogmatics, as a testimony against the pagan-philosophical
view of the eternity of the world and the efficient operations of Nature. What we perceive of the sensible world,
— say these Atomists, — is made up of passing 'accidents'
which every moment come and go. The substratum of this
'change' is constituted by the (bodily) substances; and because of changes occurring in or on these substances, they
cannot be thought of as themselves unchangeable. If then
they are changeable, they cannot be permanent, for that
which is eternal does not change. Consequently everything
in the world, since everything changes, has come into being,
or has been created by God.

That is the starting-point. The changeableness of all that
exists argues an eternal, unchangeable Creator. But later
writers, under the influence of Muslim philosophers, infer
from the possible or contingent character of everything finite,
the necessary existence of God.

But let us come back to the world. It consists of Accidents and their substrata, — Substances. Substance and Accident or Quality are the two categories by means of which reality is conceived. The remaining categories 'either come under the category of Quality, or else are resolved into relations, and modifications of thought, to which, objectively, nothing corresponds. Matter, as possibility, exists only in thought: Time is nothing other than the coexistence of different objects, or simultaneity in presentation; and Space and Size may be attributed to bodies indeed, but not to the individual parts (Atoms), of which bodies are composed.

But, generally speaking, it is Accidents which form the proper predicates of substances. Their number in every individual substance is very great, or even infinite as some maintain, since of any pair whatever of opposite determinations, — and these include negatives also, — the one or the other is attributable to every substance. The negative 'accident' is just as real as the positive. God creates also Privation and Annihilation, though certainly it is not easy to discover a substratum for these. And seeing that no Accident can ever have its place elsewhere than in some substance, and cannot have it in another Accident, there is really nothing general or common in any number of substances. Universals in no wise exist in individual things: They are Concepts.

Thus there is no connection between substances: they stand apart, in their capacity of atoms equal to one another. In fact they have a greater resemblance to the Homoeomeries of Anaxagoras than to the extremely small particles of matter of the Atomists. In themselves they are

non-spatial (without *makan*), but they have their position
(*hayyiz*), and by means of this position of theirs they fill
space. It is thus unities not possessing extension, but conceived of as points, — out of which the spatial world of
body is constructed. Between these unities there must be
a void, for were it otherwise any motion would be impossible, since the atoms do not press upon one another.
All change, however, is referred to Union and Separation,
Movement and Rest. Farther operative relations between
the Atom-substances, there are none. The Atoms exist then,
and enjoy their existence, but have nothing at all to do
with one another. The world is a discontinuous mass, without any living reciprocal action between its parts.

The ancients had prepared the way for this conception
by their theory, amongst other things, of the discontinuous
character of Number. Was not Time defined as the tale
or numbering of Motion? Why should we not apply
that doctrine to Space, Time and Motion? The Dialecticians
did this; and the 'skepsis' of the older philosophy may
have contributed its influence in the process. Like the substantial, corporeal world, — Space, Time and Motion were
decomposed into atoms devoid of extension, and into moments without duration. Time becomes a succession of many
individual 'Nows', and between every two moments of time
there is a void. The same is the case with Motion: between every two movements there is a Rest. A quick motion
and a slow motion possess the same speed, but the latter
has more points of Rest. Then, in order to get over the
difficulty of the empty space, the unoccupied moment of
time, and the pause for rest between two movements, the
theory of a Leap is made use of. Motion is to be regarded

as a leaping onward from one point in space to another, and Time as an advance effected in the same manner from one moment to another.

In reality they had no use at all for this fantastic theory of a Leap: it was a mere reply to unsophisticated questioning. With perfect consistency they had cut up the entire material world, as it moves in space and time, into Atoms with their Accidents. Some no doubt maintained, that although accidents every moment disappear, yet substances endure, but others made no difference in this respect. They taught that substances, which are in fact points in space, exist only for a point of time, just like Accidents. Every moment God creates the world anew, so that its condition at the present moment has no essential connection with that which has immediately preceded it or that which follows next. In this way there is a series of worlds following one another, which merely present the appearance of one world. That for us there is anything like connection or Causality in phenomena proceeds from the fact that Allah in his inscrutable will does not choose either to-day or to-morrow to interrupt the usual course of events by a miracle, — which however he is able at any moment to do. The disappearance of all causal connection according to the Atomistic Kalam is vividly illustrated by the classical instance of 'the writing man.' God creates in him, — and that too by an act of creation which is every moment renewed — first the will, then the faculty of writing, next the movement of the hand, and lastly the motion of the pen. Here one thing is completely independent of the other.

Now if against this view the objection is urged, that along with Causality or the regular succession of worldly events, the possibility of any knowledge is taken away, the believing thinker replies, that Allah verily foreknows everything, and creates not only the things of the world and what they appear to effect, but also the knowledge about them in the human soul, and we do not need to be wiser than He. He knows best.

Allah and the World, God and Man, — beyond these antitheses Muslim dialectic could not reach. Besides God, there is room only for corporeal substances and their accidents. The existence of human souls as incorporeal substances, as well as generally the existence of pure Spirits, — both of which doctrines were maintained by philosophers, and, though less definitely, by several Mutazilites, — would not harmonize properly with the Muslim doctrine of the transcendent nature of God, who has no associate. The soul belongs to the world of body. Life, Sensation, Rational endowment, are accidents, just as much as Colour, Taste, Smell, Motion and Rest. Some assume only one soul-atom: According to others several finer soul-atoms are mingled with the bodily atoms. At all events thinking is attached to one single Atom.

13. It was not every good Muslim that could find mental repose in dialectic. The pious servant of God might yet, in another way, draw somewhat nearer to his Lord. This need, — existing in Islam at the very outset, strengthened too by Christian and Indo-Persian influences, and intensified under more highly developed conditions of civilization, — evoked in Islam a series of phenomena, which are usually designated as Mysticism or Sufism. [1] In this development of a Muslim order of Holy men, or of a Muslim Monkish

---

[1] Ascetics were called *Sufis*, from their coarse woollen garment, or *Sûf*

system, the history of Christian monks and cloisters in Syria and Egypt, as well as that of Indian devotees, is repeated. In this matter then we have at bottom to deal with religious or spiritual practice; but practice always mirrors itself in thought, and receives its theory. In order to bring about a more intimate relationship with the Godhead, many symbolical acts and mediating persons were required. Such persons then endeavoured to discover the mysteries of the symbols for themselves and to disclose them to the initiated, and to establish, besides, their own mediatory position in the scale of universal being. In particular, Neo-Platonic doctrines, — partly drawn from the turbid source of the Pseudo-Dionysius the Areopagite and the holy Hierotheos (Stephen bar Sudaili?) — had to lend their aid in this work. The Indian Yoga too, at least in Persia, seems to have exercised considerable influence. For the most part Mysticism kept within the pale of Orthodoxy, which was always sensible enough to allow a certain latitude to poets and enthusiasts. As regards the doctrine that God *works* all in all, Dialecticians and Mystics were agreed; but extreme Mysticism propounded the farther doctrine that God *is* all in all. From this a heterodox Pantheism was developed, which made the world an empty show, and deified the human Ego. Thus the Unity of God becomes Universal Unity; his universal activity Universal Existence. Besides God, there exist at the most only the attributes and conditions of the Sufi souls that are tending towards him. A psychology of feeling is developed by the Sufi teachers. In their view, while our conceptions come to the soul from without, and our exertions amount to the externalizing of what is within, the true essence of our soul consists in certain states or feelings of inclination and disinclination. The most essential of all these is Love. It is neither fear nor hope, but Love that lifts us up to God. Blessedness is not a matter of 'knowing' or of 'willing': it is Union with the loved one. These Mystics did away with the world (as ultimately they did with the human soul) in a far more thorough-going fashion than the Dialecticians had done. By the latter the world was sacrificed to the arbitrary character of God in Creation; by the former to the illuminating, loving nature of the Divine Being. The confusing multiplicity of things, as that appears to sense and conception, is removed in a yearning after the One and Beloved being. Everything, both in Being and Thinking, is brought to one central point. Contrast with this the genuine Greek spirit. In it a wish was cherished for a still greater number of senses, to enable men to get a somewhat better acquaintance with this fair world. But these Mystics blame the senses for being too many, because their number brings disorder into their felicity.

Human nature, however, always asserts herself. Those men who renounce the world and the senses, frequently run riot in the most sensual fantasies, till far advanced in life. We need not wonder after all, that many troubled themselves very little indeed about religious doctrine, or that the ascetic morality of the Sufis often went to the other extreme.

The task of following out in detail the development of Sufism, however, belongs to the history of Religion rather than to the history of Philosophy. Besides, we find the philosophical elements which it took up, in the Muslim philosophers whom we shall meet with farther on.

4. Literature and History.

1. Arabic Poetry and Annalistic were developed independently of the learning of the schools. But as time went on, Literature and Historical Composition could not remain untouched by foreign influences. A few notices, confirmatory of this statement, must suffice us here.

The introduction of Islam involved no break with the poetical tradition of the Arab race, such as had been occasioned by Christianity in the Teutonic world. The secular literature of the times even of the Omayyads handed down many wise sayings, partly taken from ancient Arabic poetry, which rivalled the preachings of the Koran. Abbasid Caliphs, like Mansur, Harun and Mamun, had more literary culture than Charlemagne. The education of their sons was not confined to the reading of the Koran: it embraced acquaintance also with the ancient poets and with the history of the nation. Poets and literary men were drawn to the courts and rewarded in princely fashion. In these circumstances, Literature underwent the influence of scholarly culture and philosophical speculation, although, in most cases, in a very superficial manner. The result is specially exhibited in sceptical utterances, frivolous mockery of what is most sacred, and glorification of sensual pleasure. At the same time, however, wise sayings, serious reflections and mystic speculations made their way into the originally sober and realistic poetry of the Arabs. The place of the first natural freshness of representation was now taken by a wearisome play on thoughts and sentiments, and even on mere words, metres and rhymes.

2. The unpleasant Abu-l-Atahia (748—828), in his effeminate poetry, is nearly always talking about unhappy

love and a longing for death. He gives expression to his
wisdom in the following couplet:

"The mind guide thou with cautious hesitation:
'Gainst sin use the best shield, Renunciation".

Whoever possesses any faculty for appreciating life and
the poetry of Nature will find little to enjoy in his world-
renouncing songs; and just as little satisfaction will be afforded
him in the verses of Mutanabbi (905—965), frightfully
tedious in their contents, although epigrammatic in their
form. And yet Mutanabbi has been praised as the greatest
Arabic poet.

In like manner people have unduly extolled Abu-l-Ala
al-Maarri (973—1058) as a philosophic poet. His occasionally
quite respectable sentiments and sensible views are not
philosophy, nor does the affected though often hackneyed
expression of these amount to poetry. Under more favourable conditions, — for he was blind and not surpassingly
rich, — this man might perhaps have rendered some service
in the subordinate walks of criticism as a philologist or a
historical writer. But, in place of an enthusiastic acceptance
of life's duties, he is led to preach the joyless abandonment
of them, and to grumble generally at political conditions,
the opinions of the orthodox multitude, and the scientific
assertions of the learned, without being able himself to
advance anything positive. He is almost entirely wanting
in the gift of combination. He can analyse, but he does
not hit upon any synthesis, and his learning bears no fruit.
The tree of his knowledge has its roots in the air, as he
himself confesses in one of his letters, though in a different
sense. He leads a life of strict celibacy and vegetarianism,

as becomes a pessimist. As he puts it in his poems "all is but an idle toy: Fate is blind; and Time spares neither the king who partakes of the joys of life, nor the devout man who spends his nights in watching and prayer. Nor does irrational belief solve for us the enigma of existence. Whatever is behind those moving heavens remains hidden from us for ever: Religions, which open up a prospect there, have been fabricated from motives of self-interest. Sects and factions of all kinds are utilized by the powerful to make their dominion secure, though the truth about these matters can only be whispered. The wisest thing then is to keep aloof from the world, and to do good disinterestedly, and because it is virtuous and noble to do so, without any outlook for reward".

Other literary men had a more practical philosophy, and could make their weight more felt in the world. They subscribed to the wise doctrine of the Theatre-Manager in Goethe's Faust: "He who brings much, will something bring to many". The most perfect type of this species is Hariri (1054—1122), whose hero, the beggar and stroller, Abu Zaid of Serug, teaches as the highest wisdom:

> "Hunt, instead of being hunted;
> All the world's a wood for hunting.
> If the falcon should escape you,
> Take, content, the humble bunting:
> If you finger not the dinars,
> Coppers still are worth the counting" [1].

3. The Annalistic of the ancient Arabs, like their Poetry, was distinguished by a clear perception of particulars, but

---

[1] *V.* Rückerts Uebers. d. Makamen II, p. 219.

was incapable of taking a general grasp of events. With
the vast extension of the empire their view was necessarily
widened. First a great mass of material was gathered together. Their historical and geographical knowledge was
advanced by means of journeys undertaken to collect traditions, or for purposes of administration and trade, or simply
to satisfy curiosity, more than it could have been by mere
religious pilgrimages. Characteristic methods of research,
brought to bear upon the value of tradition as a source
of our knowledge, were elaborated. With the same subtlety
which they displayed in Grammar, they portioned out,
in endless division and subdivision, the extended field of
their observation, in a fashion more truly 'arabesque' than
lucid; and in this way they formed a logic of history
which must have appeared to an oriental eye much finer
than the Aristotelian Organon with its austere structure.
Their tradition, — in authenticating which they were, as
a rule, less particular in practice than in theory, — was
by many made equal in value to the evidence of the senses,
and preferred to the judgment of the reason, which so
easily admitted fallacious inferences.

There were always people, however, who impartially handed
down contradictory reports, alongside of one another. Others,
although exhibiting consideration for the feelings and requirements of the present, did not withhold their more or
less well-founded judgment on the past, for it is often easier
to be discerning in matters of history than in the affairs
of the living world.

New subjects of enquiry came up, together with new
modes of treatment. Geography included somewhat of Natural
Philosophy, for example in the geography of climate; while

historical composition brought within the range of its description intellectual life, belief, morals, literature and science. Acquaintance also with other lands and nations invited comparison on many points; and thus an international, humanistic or cosmopolitan element was introduced.

4. A representative of the humanistic attitude of mind is met with in Masudi, who died about the year 956. He appreciates, and is interested in, everything that concerns humanity. Everywhere he is learning something from the men he meets with: and in consequence the reading of books, which occupies his privacy, is not without fruit. But it is neither the narrow, everyday practices of life and religion, nor the airy speculations of Philosophy, that specially appeal to him. He knows where his strength lies; and up to the last, when he is spending his old age in Egypt, far from his native home, he finds his consolation, — the medicine of his soul, — - in the study of History. History for him is the all-embracing science: it is his philosophy; and its task is to set forth the truth of that which was and is. Even the wisdom of the world, together with its development, becomes the subject of History; and without it all knowledge would long since have disappeared. For learned men come and go; but History records their intellectual achievements, and thereby restores the connection between the past and the present. It gives us unprejudiced information about events and about the views of men. Of course Masudi leaves it often to the intelligent reader to find out for himself the due synthesis of the facts and the individual opinion of the author.

A successor of his, the geographer Maqdasi, or Muqaddasi, who wrote in the year 985, deserves to be mentioned with high commendation. He journeyed through many countries, and exercised the most varied callings, in order to acquaint himself with the life of his time. He is a true Abu Zaid of Serug (cf. II, 4 § 2), but one with an object before him.

He sets to work in critical fashion, and holds to the knowledge which is gained by research and enquiry, not by faith in tradition or by mere deductions of the reason. The geographical statements in the Koran he explains by the limited intellectual horizon of the ancient Arabs, to which Allah must have seen fit to adapt himself.

He describes then, *sine ira et studio*, the countries and races he has seen with own eyes. His plan is to set down, in the first place, results gathered from his own experience and observation; next, what he has heard from trustworthy people; and last of all what he has met with in books. The following sentences are extracted from his characterization of himself.

"I have given instruction in the common subjects of education and morals: I have come forward as a preacher, and I have made the minaret of the mosque resound with the call to prayer. I have been present at the meetings of the learned and the devotions of the pious. I have partaken of broth with Sufis, gruel with monks, and ship's-fare with sailors. Many a time I have been seclusion itself, and then again I have eaten forbidden fruit against my better judgment. I associated with the hermits of Lebanon, and in turn I lived at the court of the Prince. In wars I have participated: I have been detained as a captive and thrown into prison as a spy. Powerful princes and ministers have lent me their ear, and anon I have joined a band of robbers, or sat as a retail-dealer in the bazaar. I have enjoyed much honour and consideration, but I have likewise been fated to listen to many curses and to be reduced to the ordeal of the oath, when I was suspected of heresy or evil deeds".

We are accustomed at the present day to picture to ourselves the Oriental as a being who, in contemplative repose, is completely bound to his ancestral faith and usages. This representation is not quite correct, but still it agrees better with the situation which now exists than it does with the disposition of Islam in the first four centuries, for during that period it was inclined to take into its possession not only the outward advantages of the world, but also the intellectual acquisitions of Mankind.

III. THE PYTHAGOREAN PHILOSOPHY.

1. NATURAL PHILOSOPHY.

1. Euclid and Ptolemy, Hippocrates and Galen, some portion of Aristotle, and, in addition, an abundant Neo-Platonic Literature, — indicate the elements of Arabic Natural Philosophy. It is a popular philosophy, which, chiefly through the instrumentality of the Sabaeans of Harran, found acceptance with the Shi'ites and other sects, and which in due course impressed not only court circles, but also a large body of educated and half-educated people. Stray portions of it were taken from the writings of the "Logician", — Aristotle, — e. g. from the "Meteorology", from the work "On the Universe", which has been attributed to him, from the "Book of Animals", from the "Psychology", and so on; but its general character was determined by Pythagorean-Platonic teaching, by the Stoics, and by subsequent astrologers and alchemists. Human curiosity and piety were fain to read the secrets of the Deity in the book of his Creation, and they proceeded in this search far beyond practical requirements, which merely called for a little arithmetic to serve in the division of inheritances and in trade, and a little astronomy besides, to determine the proper times for celebrating the functions of religion.

Men hastened to gather wisdom from every quarter, and in so doing they manifested a conviction, which Masudi accurately expressed, when he said: "Whatever is good should be recognized, whether it is found in friend or foe". Indeed Ali, the prince of believers, is reported to have said: "The wisdom of the world is the believer's strayed sheep: take it back, even though it come from the unbelieving".

Pythagoras is the presiding genius of Mathematical study in Islam. Greek and Indian elements are mingled in it, it is true, but everything is regarded from a Neo-Pythagorean point of view. Without studying such branches of Mathematics, as Arithmetic and Geometry, Astronomy and Music, no one, they said, becomes a philosopher or an educated physician. The Theory of Numbers, — prized more highly than Mensuration, because it appeals less to the outward vision, and should bring the mind nearer the essence of things, — gave occasion to the most extravagant puerilities. God is, of course, the great Unity, from whom everything proceeds, who himself is no number, but who is the First Cause of Number. But above all, the number Four, — the number of the elements and so on, — was held in high favour by the philosophers; and by-and-by nothing in heaven or earth was spoken of or written about, except in sentences of four clauses and in discourses under four heads.

The transition from Mathematics to Astronomy and Astrology was rapid and easy. The old Eastern methods, which came into their hands, continued to be applied even by the court-astrologers of the Omayyads, but with still greater thoroughness at the Abbasid court. In this way

they arrived at speculations which ran counter to the revealed Faith, and which therefore could never be approved
of by the guardians of religion. The only antithesis which
existed for the Believer was — God and the World, or
this life and the next; but for the Astrologer there were
two worlds, one of the Heavens and another of the Earth,
while God and the life beyond were in the far distance.
According to the different conceptions entertained of the
relation which subsisted between the heavenly bodies and
sublunary things, either a rational Astronomy was developed, or a fantastic Astrology. Only a few kept entirely
free from Astrological delusions. As long, in fact, as the
science was dominated by the Ptolemaic system, it was
easier for the completely uneducated man to jeer at what
was absurd in it than it was for the learned investigator
to disprove the same. For the latter indeed this earth with
its forms of life was a product of the forces of the heavens,
a reflection of celestial light, an echo of the eternal harmony
of the Spheres. Those then who ascribed conception and
will to the Spirits of the stars and spheres, held them
as the representatives of Divine providence, and thus traced
to their agency both what is good and what is evil, seeking
also to foretell future events from the situation of their
orbs, by means of which they bring their influence to bear
upon earthly things in accordance with steadfast laws. Others,
it is true, had their doubts about this secondary providence,
on grounds of experience and reason, or from the Peripatetic
belief that the blessed existences of the heavens are Spirits
of pure intellect, exalted above conception and will, and
in consequence above all particularity that appeals to the
senses, so that their providential influence is directed only

to the good of the whole, but never can have reference to any individual occurrence.

3. In the domain of Natural Science Muslim learned men collected a rich body of material; but hardly in any case did they succeed in really treating it scientifically. In the separate Natural sciences, the development of which we cannot follow up in this place, they clung to traditional systems. To establish the wisdom of God and the operations of Nature, — which was regarded as a power or emanation of the World-Soul, — alchemistic experiments were instituted, the magical virtues of talismans tested, the effects of Music upon the emotions of men and animals investigated, and observations made on physiognomy, while attempts were also set on foot to explain the wonders of the life of sleep and of dreams, as well as those of soothsaying and prophecy, &c. As might be expected, the centre of interest was Man, as the Microcosm which must combine in itself all the elements and powers of the world together. The essential part of Man's being was held to be the Soul; and its relation to the World-Soul, and its future lot were made subjects of enquiry. There was also a good deal of speculation about the faculties of the soul and their localization in the heart and the brain. One or two adhered to Galen, but others went farther than he did, and made out five inner senses corresponding to the five outer ones, — a theory which, along with similar natural mysteries, was traced to Apollonius of Tyana.

Obviously the most diverse attitudes towards religious doctrine were possible in the study of Mathematical and Physical Science. But the propaedeutic sciences, as soon as they came forward on their own account, were always

dangerous to the Faith. The assumption of the eternity of
the world, and of an uncreated matter in motion from
all eternity, — was readily combined with Astronomy. And
if the movement of the Heavens is eternal, so too are, no
doubt, the changes which take place on earth. All the kingdoms of Nature then, according to many teachers, being
eternal, the race of man is eternal also, wheeling round
and round in an orbit of its own. There is therefore nothing
new in the world : the views and ideas of men repeat themselves like everything else. All that can possibly be done,
maintained or known, has already been and will again be.

Admirable discourse and lamentation were expended upon
this theme, without much advancing thereby the interests
of Science.

4. The science of Medicine, which on obvious grounds
was favoured by the ruling powers, appears to have proved
somewhat more useful. Its interests furnished one of the
reasons, and not the least considerable, which induced
the Caliphs to commission so many men to translate Greek
authors. It is therefore not to be wondered at that the
teachings of Mathematics and Natural Science, together with
Logic, also affected Medicine intimately. The old-fashioned
doctor was disposed to be satisfied with time-honoured
magical formulae, and other empirical expedients; but
modern society in the ninth century required philosophical
knowledge in the physician. He had to know the "natures"
of foods, stimulants or luxuries, and medicaments, the
humours of the body, and in every case the influence of
the stars. The physician was brother to the astrologer,
whose knowledge commanded his respect, because it had
a more exalted object than medical practice. He had to

attend the lectures of the alchemist, and to practise his art in accordance with the methods of Mathematics and Logic. It was not enough for the fanatics of education in the ninth century that a man had to speak, believe and behave in accordance with *Qiyas*, — that is to say, with logical correctness: he must, over and above, submit to be treated medically in accordance with *Qiyas*. The principles of Medicine were discussed in learned assemblies at the court of Wathik (842—847) like the foundations of Doctrine and Morals. The question, in fact, was asked, prompted by a work of Galen's, whether Medicine relies upon tradition, experience or rational knowledge, or whether on the other hand it derives its support from the principles of Mathematics and Natural Science by means of logical deduction (*Qiyas*).

5. The Natural Philosophy, which has just been rapidly sketched, actually stood for Philosophy with the most of the scholars of the ninth century, as contrasted with theological dialectic, and was styled Pythagorean. It lasted even into the tenth century, when its most important representative was the famous physician Razi († 923 or 932). Born in Rai he received a mathematical education and studied Medicine and Natural Philosophy with great diligence. He was averse to dialectic and was only acquainted with Logic as far as the categorical figures of the First Analytics. After having practised as director of the hospital in his native city and in Bagdad, he entered upon his travels and resided at various princely courts, amongst others at the court of the Samanid Mansur ibn Ishaq, to whom he dedicated a work on Medicine.

Razi has a high opinion of the medical profession and of the study which it demands. The wisdom of a thousand

years, contained in books, he prizes more than the experiences of the individual man gained in one short life, but
he prefers even these to deductions of the "Logicians" which
have not been tested by experience.

He thinks that the relation between the body and the
soul is determined by the soul. And seeing that in this
way the circumstances and sufferings of the soul admit of
being discerned by means of the physiognomy, the medical
man has to be at the same time a physician of the soul.
Therefore he drew up a system of spiritual medicine, —
a kind of Dietetic of the Soul. The precepts of Muslim
law, like the prohibition of wine, and so on, gave him no
concern, but his freethinking seems to have led him into
pessimism. In fact he found more evil than good in the
world, and described inclination as the absence of disinclination.

High though the value was which Razi put upon Aristotle
and Galen, he did not give himself any special trouble to
gain a more profound comprehension of their works. He
was a devoted student of Alchemy, which in his view was
a true art, based on the existence of a primeval matter,
— an art indispensable to philosophers, and which, he
believed, had been practised by Pythagoras, Democritus,
Plato, Aristotle and Galen. In opposition to Peripatetic
teaching he assumed that the body contained in itself the
principle of movement, a thought which might certainly
have proved a fruitful one in Natural Science, if it had
been recognized and farther developed.

Razi's Metaphysic starts from old doctrines, which his
contemporaries ascribed to Anaxagoras, Empedocles, Mani
and others. At the apex of his system stand five co-eternal

principles, — the Creator, the Universal Soul, the First or Primeval matter, Absolute Space, and Absolute Time or Eternal Duration. In these the necessary conditions of the actually existing world are given. The individual sense-perceptions, generally, presuppose an existing Matter, just as the grouping of different perceived objects postulates Space. Perceptions of change farther constrain us to assume the condition of Time. The existence of living beings leads us to recognize a Soul; and the fact that some of these living beings are endowed with Reason, *i. e.* — have the faculty of bringing the Arts to the highest perfection, — necessitates our belief in a wise Creator, whose Reason has ordered everything for the best.

Notwithstanding the eternity of his five principles, Razi thus speaks of a Creator and even gives a story of Creation. First then a simple, pure, spiritual Light was created, the material of Souls, which are simple, spiritual substances, of the nature of Light. That Light-material or Upper-world, from which souls descended, is also called Reason, or Light of the Light of God. The Light is followed by the Shadow, from which the Animal Soul is created, for the service of the Rational Soul. But simultaneously with the simple, spiritual light, there existed from the first a composite form, which is Body, from the shadow of which now issue the four "natures", Warmth and Cold, Dryness and Moistness. From these four natures at last are formed all heavenly and earthly bodies. The whole process, however, is in operation from all eternity, without beginning in time, for God was never inactive.

That Razi was an astrologer is plain from his own utterances. The heavenly bodies consist indeed, according to him, of the same elements as earthly things, and the latter are continually exposed to the influences of the former.

6. Razi had to maintain a polemical attitude in two directions. On the one side he impugned the Muslim Unity of God, which could not bear to be associated with any eternal soul, matter, space or time; and on the other side he attacked the Dahrite system, which does not acknowledge any Creator of the world. This system, which is frequently mentioned by Muslim authors, with due aversion of course, appears to have found numerous representatives, though none of any importance. The adherents of the 'Dahr' (v. I, 2, § 2) are represented to us as Materialists, Sensualists, Atheists, Believers in the transmigration of souls, and so on; but we learn nothing more definite about their doctrines. In any case the Dahrites had no need to trace all that exists to a principle which was of spiritual essence and creative efficiency. Muslim Philosophy, on the other hand, did stand in need of such a principle, if it should only conform in some degree to the teaching of the faith. Natural Philosophy was not suited for the furtherance of this object, as it showed more interest in the manifold and often contrary operations of Nature than in the One Cause of all. Such aim was better attained by Neo-Platonic Aristotelianism, whose logico-metaphysical speculations endeavoured to trace all existence to one highest existence, or to derive all things from one supreme operative principle. But before we attend to this direction of thought, which commenced to appear even in the ninth century, we have still to give some account of an attempt to blend Natural Philosophy and the teachings of the Faith into a Philosophy of Religion.

2. The Faithful Brethren of Basra.

1. In the East, where every religion formed a State within the State, a political party invariably made its appearance in the additional character of a religious sect, just to gain adherents in some way or other. As a matter of principle indeed, Islam knew no distinction between men, — no caste or social standing. But property and education have the same influence everywhere; and in their train degrees of piety and stages of knowledge began to be set up, according as a community or party permitted of adjustment. Thus there arose secret societies having different grades, of which the highest and perhaps the next highest possessed an esoteric doctrine, which borrowed a good deal from the Natural Philosophy of the Neo-Pythagoreans. In furtherance of their object, which was to conquer political power, every expedient was regarded as lawful. For the initiated the Koran was explained allegorically. They traced their mystic lore, it is true, back to prophets with Biblical and Koranic names, but heathen philosophers were at the bottom of it all. Philosophy was completely transformed into a mythology of politics. The high intelligences and souls, which theoretic thinkers had recognized in the stars and planets, embodied themselves in human beings for the work of actual Politics; and it was declared to be a religious duty to assist these embodied intelligences in the establishment of an earthly kingdom of righteousness. The associations which acted in this way may best be compared to societies, which up to the days of Saint-Simonism and kindred phenomena in last century were wont to appear in countries where freedom of thought was restricted.

In the second half of the ninth century Abdallah ibn
Maimun, head of the Karmatite party, was the originator
of a movement of this kind. He was a Persian oculist,
trained in the school of the Natural Philosophers. He
proved able to associate both believers and freethinkers in
a confederacy to endeavour to compass the overthrow of
the Abbasid government. To the one set he was a con-
jurer, to the other a pious ascetic or learned philosopher.
His colours were white, because his religion was that of
the pure light, to which the soul was to ascend after its
earthly wanderings. The duties inculcated were contempt
for the body, disregard of the Material, community of
goods for all the confederate brethren, as well as self-
surrender to the confederacy, and fidelity and obedience to
their chiefs, even to death, — for the society had its grades.
In accordance with the sequence of existence, viz., God,
Reason, Soul, Space and Time, they conceived the revelation of God to be made in history and in the constitution of their own brotherhood.

2. The chief homes of Karmatite activity were Basra
and Kufa. Now we find in Basra in the second half of
the tenth century a small association of men, whose confederacy aims at having four grades. We do not know, to
be sure, how far the brethren succeeded in realizing the
ideal organization of their confederacy. To the first grade
belong young men of from 15 to 30 years of age, whose
souls are being formed in the natural way: these must
be completely submissive to their teachers. The second
grade, — from 30 to 40 years of age — are introduced
to secular wisdom, and receive an analogical knowledge of
things. In the third grade, — from 40 to 50 years of

age — the Divine law of the world becomes known in more adequate form: that constitutes the stage of the prophets. Finally, in the highest grade, when one is over 50 years old, he comes to see the true reality of things, just like the blessed angels: he is exalted then above Nature, Doctrine and Law.

From this brotherhood there has come down to us a progressively-advancing Encyclopaedia of the Sciences of that day. It consists of 51 (originally perhaps 50) treatises, the contents of which are of such varied nature and origin that the redactors or compilers have not succeeded in establishing a complete harmony among them. In general, however, there is found in this Encyclopaedia an eclectic Gnosticism built on a foundation of Natural Science, and provided with a political background. The scheme sets out with mathematical considerations, continually playing with numbers and letters, and proceeds through Logic and Physics, — referring everything, however, to the Soul and its powers, — in order to approach at last, in a mystical and magical fashion, the knowledge of the Godhead. The whole representation is that of the doctrine of a persecuted sect, with the political features peeping out here and there. We see also something of suffering and struggle, — something of the oppressions to which the men of this Encyclopaedia or their predecessors were exposed, and something of the hope they cherished and the patience they preached. They seek in this spiritualistic philosophy, consolation or redemption: It is their religion. 'Faithful to death,' — so runs the expression — shall the brethren be, for to meet death for a friend's welfare, is the true Holy war. In life's pilgrimage through this world, —

thus the obligatory journey to Mecca is allegorized —, one must aid the other by all the means in his power. The rich must communicate to others a share of their material goods, and the wise a share of their intellectual possessions. But yet knowledge, as we have it in the Encyclopaedia, was probably reserved for initiated members of the highest grade.

It must be allowed, however, that this confraternity of the Faithful Brethren of Basra seems to have led a quiet existence, as perhaps was the case also with a branch-settlement of theirs in Bagdad. The relation of the Brethren to the Karmatites may have resembled that of the more peaceful Baptists to the revolutionary Anabaptists of the 'King of Sion'. [1]

The names of the following have been given to us by later writers, as having been members of the Brotherhood and collaborators of the Encyclopaedia, viz.: Abu Sulaiman Mohammed ibn Mushir al-Busti, called al-Muqaddasi; Abu-l-Hasan Ali ibn Harun al-Zandjani; Mohammed ibn Akhmed al-Nahradjuri; Al-Aufi and Zaid ibn Rifaa. In the time of their activity the Caliphate had already been forced to make an entire surrender of its secular power into the hands of the Shi'ite dynasty of the Buyids. Probably this circumstance was favourable to the appearance of an Encyclopaedia, in which Shi'ite and Mutazilite doctrines together with the results of Philosophy were comprehended in one popular system.

3. The Brethren themselves avow their eclecticism. They wish to collect the wisdom of all nations and religions. Noah and Abraham, Socrates and Plato, Zoroaster and

---

[1] [*Translator's note.* — 'John of Leyden'].

Jesus, Mohammed and Ali are all prophets of theirs. Socrates, and Jesus and his apostles, no less than the children of Ali, are honoured as holy martyrs of their rational faith. The religious law in its literal sense is pronounced good for the ordinary man, — a medicine for weak and ailing souls: the deeper philosophic insight is for strong intelligences. Though the body is devoted to death, dying means rising again to the pure life of the Spirit, for those who during their earthly existence have been awakened by means of philosophic considerations out of careless slumber and foolish sleep. This is impressed with endless repetition, by means of legends and myths of later-Greek, Judaeo-Christian, Persian or Indian origin. Every transitory thing is here turned into an emblem. On the ruins of positive religion and unsophisticated opinion a spiritualistic philosophy is built up, embracing all the knowledge and endeavour of human kind, so far as these came within the Brethren's field of view. The aim of their philosophizing is given as 'the assimilation of the soul to God, in the degree possible for man'.

In this scheme, the negative tendencies of the Brethren, are kept somewhat in the background, for reasons which are quite intelligible. But their criticism of human society and of positive religions is exhibited with least reserve in the 'Book of the Animal and the Man', in which the figurative dress makes it possible for them to represent animals as saying what might be questionable if heard from a human mouth.

4. The eclectic character of the scheme, and the far from systematic method adopted in its subdivisions render it difficult to give a coherent exposition of the philosophy

of the Brethren. But still the most important tenets, though sometimes loosely connected, must here be set forth with a measure of order.

The mental activity of Man falls to be divided, according to the Encyclopaedia, into Art and Science. Now Science or Knowledge is the form assumed within the knowing soul by that which is known, or a higher, finer, more intellectual mode of existence of whatever is realized in outward substance. Art on the other hand consists in projecting the form from the artist-soul into matter. Knowledge is potentially present in the soul of the disciple, but it becomes actual only through the teaching activity of a master, who carries knowledge as a reality within his own mind. But whence did it come to the first master? The Brethren answer, that according to the philosophers he gained it by his own reflection, while, according to the theologians, he received it through prophetic illumination; "but in our view there are various ways or instrumentalities by which knowledge may be attained. From the intermediate position of the soul, between the worlds of body and of mind it results that there are open to it three ways or sources of knowledge. Thus by means of the senses the soul is made acquainted with what is beneath it, and through logical inference with what is above it, and finally with itself by rational consideration or direct intuition. Of these kinds of knowledge the surest and the most deserving of preference is knowledge of one's self. When human knowledge attempts to go farther than this, it proves itself to be limited in many ways. Therefore one must not philosophize straight away about questions like the origin or the eternity of the world, but make his first essays with what is simpler. And only·

through renunciation of the world, and righteous conduct, does the soul lift itself gradually up to the pure knowledge of the Highest."

5. After secular instruction in Grammar, Poetry and History, and after religious education and doctrine, philosophic study should begin with the mathematical branches. Here everything is set forth in Neo-Pythagorean and Indian fashion. Not only numbers but even the letters of the alphabet are employed in childish trifling. It was particularly convenient for the Brethren that the number of letters in the Arabic alphabet is 28, or 4 multiplied by 7. Instead of proceeding according to practical and real points of view, they give the rein to fancy in all the sciences, in accordance with grammatical analogies and relations of numbers. Their Arithmetic does not investigate Number as such, but rather its significance. No search is made for any more suitable mode of expressing number in the case of phenomena; but things are themselves explained in accordance with the system of numbers. The Theory of number is Divine wisdom, and is above Things, for things are only formed after the pattern of numbers. The absolute principle of all existence and thought is the number One. The science of number, therefore, is found at the beginning, middle, and end of all philosophy. Geometry, with its figures addressing the eye, serves merely to make it more easily understood by beginners, but Arithmetic alone is true and pure science. And yet Geometry too is divided into a sensible form of it which deals with lines, surfaces and solids, and a pure or spiritual form which treats of the dimensions or properties of things, such as length, breadth and depth. The object both of Arithmetic and

Geometry is to conduct the soul from the sensible to the spiritual.

First of all then they lead us to consider the stars. Now the Encylopaedia offers us, in its Astrology, — and nothing else could be expected — teaching which is exceedingly fantastic and sometimes self-contradictory. The whole of it is pervaded by the conviction that the stars not merely foretell the future, but directly influence or bring about every thing that happens beneath the moon. Fortune and misfortune come equally from them. Jupiter, Venus and the Sun bring fortune; misfortune is brought, on the other hand, by Saturn, Mars and the Moon; while the effects produced by the planet Mercury have in them both bad and good. Mercury is the lord of education and science: we owe to him our knowledge, which comprises bad and good. In the same way too the other planets have all their several spheres of influence; and man in the course of life, if he is not prematurely snatched away, experiences successively the influences of the whole of the heavenly bodies. The Moon causes his body to grow and Mercury forms his mind. Then he comes under the sway of Venus. The Sun gives him family, riches or dominion; Mars, bravery and noble-mindedness. Thereupon, under the guidance of Jupiter, he prepares, by means of religious exercises, for the journey to the world beyond, and he attains rest under the influence of Saturn. Many men, however, do not live long enough, or are not enabled by circumstances, to develope their natural capacities in unbroken sequence. God therefore graciously sends them his prophets, by whose teaching they may, even in a short time and under unfavourable circumstances, form their natures completely.

6. According to the Encyclopaedia, Logic is related to Mathematics. In fact just as Mathematics conducts from the sensible to the intellectual, so Logic takes an intermediate position between Physics and Metaphics. In Physics we have to do with bodies; in Metaphysics, with pure Spirits; but Logic treats of the ideas of the latter as well as of the representations of the former in our soul. Yet in range and importance Logic is inferior to Mathematics. For the subject of Mathematics is regarded not merely as an intermediary, but also as the essence of the All, while on the other hand Logic remains completely restricted to psychic forms as an intermediary between body and mind. Things are regulated by numbers, but our presentations and ideas by things.

The logical observations of the Brethren start from Porphyry's Introduction, and the Categories, the Hermeneutics and the Analytics of Aristotle. They present nothing original, or very little.

To the five terms of Porphyry, a sixth, — the 'Individual' — is added, no doubt for the sake of symmetry. Three of these, — Genus, Species, Individual, — are then called Objective Qualifications and three, — Difference, Property, Accident — Abstract or Conceptional Qualifications. The Categories are Genus-conceptions, of which the first is Substance, the other nine denoting its Accidents. The whole system of Concepts is farther developed by a division into species. But besides Division, there are three additional logical methods in use: Analysis, Definition and Deduction. Analysis is the method for beginners, because it permits a knowledge of what is individual. More subtle, however, as disclosing to us what is spiritual, — are

Definition and Deduction, the former investigating the essential nature of Species, and the latter that of Genera. The Senses apprise us of the existence of things; but acquaintance with the essence of things is gained by reflection. The information which is conveyed to us by the senses is small, as it were the letters of the alphabet. Of greater importance considerably are the principles of rational knowledge, just as words have more significance than letters; but the most important knowledge of all, lies in the propositions which have been derived from those principles, and which the human mind gains for itself or appropriates, in contradistinction to that knowledge which Nature or the Divine revelation has imparted to it.

7. From God, the highest Being, who is exalted above all distinctions and oppositions both of the Material and the Spiritual, the whole world is derived by the path of Emanation. If now and again a Creation is spoken of, that is only to be understood as a form of adaptation to theological language. The gradation then of the Emanations is exhibited as follows: 1. The Creative Spirit. (νοῦς, ʽaql); 2. The Passive Spirit, or the All-Soul or World-Soul; 3. The First Material; 4. The Operative Nature, a power of the World-Soul; 5. The Absolute Body, called also, the Second Material; 6. The World of the Spheres; 7. The Elements of the Sublunary World; 8. The Minerals, Plants and Animals composed of these elements. These then are the eight Essences which, — together with God, the Absolute One, who is in everything and with everything — complete the series of Original Essences corresponding to the nine Cardinal Numbers.

Spirit, Soul, Original Matter, and Nature are simple;

but with Body we enter the realm of the Composite. Here
all is composed of Matter and Form, or, — to adopt
another principle of division, — of Substance and Accident.
The first Substances are Matter and Form; the first Accidents
or Properties, Space, Motion and Time, to which in the
opinion of the Brethren may perhaps be added Tone and
Light. Matter is one; all plurality and diversity come from
the Forms. Substance is designated also as the constitutive,
material Form, while Accident is the completing, spiritual
Form. The Encyclopaedia does not express itself clearly on
these points. But in any case Substantiality is looked for
rather in the Universal than in the Particular, and Form
is put before Matter. The Substantial Form, like a spectre,
frightens off every attempt of the philosopher to investigate thoroughly the domain of the Material. The Forms
wander at their own sweet will like lords through the
lower world of Matter. No trace is discoverable of any
inner relation between Matter and Form. Not only in
thought, but also in reality they keep themselves separate.

From the account which has been given an idea may
now be formed of the story of Nature as the Brethren
viewed it. They have been represented as the Darwinists
of the tenth century, but nothing could be more inappro-
priate. The various realms of Nature, it is true, yield according to the Encyclopaedia an ascending and connected
series; but, the relation is determined not by bodily structure, but by the inner Form or Soul-Substance. The Form
wanders in mystic fashion from the lower to the higher
and *vice versa*, not in accordance with inner laws of
formation, or modified to suit external conditions, but in
accordance with the influences of the stars, and, in the

case of Man at least, in accordance with practical and theoretical behaviour. To give a history of Evolution in the modern sense of the term was very far from the thought of the Brethren. For example they expressly insist that the horse and the elephant resemble Man more than the ape does, although the bodily likeness is greater in the last-named. In fact in their system the body is a matter of quite secondary consideration: the death of the body is called the birth of the soul. The soul alone is an efficient existence, which procures the body for itself.

8. The teaching of the Brethren concerning Nature is therefore merged almost completely in Psychology. Let us confine ourselves here to the human soul. It stands in the centre of the All; and just as the World is a huge man, Man is a little world.

The human soul has emanated from the World-soul; and the souls of all individuals taken together constitute a substance which might be denominated the Absolute Man or the Spirit of Humanity. Every individual soul, however, is involved in Matter, and must gradually be formed into spirit. To that end it possesses many faculties or powers, and of these the speculative faculties are the choicest, for knowledge is the very life of the soul.

The soul of the child is at first like a white sheet of paper. What the five senses convey to it is first presented, then judged, and lastly stored up, in the front, middle, and hinder parts of the brain respectively. Through the faculty of speech and the art of writing, which make up the number of the internal senses to five, corresponding to the number of the External, the contents of Presentation are then realized.

Among the external senses, Hearing takes precedence of
Sight; for Sight, a mere slave of the moment, is occupied
with what is actually present to the sense, whereas Hearing
apprehends also what is past, and is conscious of the harmony of the tuneful spheres. Hearing and Sight constitute
the group of the intellectual senses, whose effect must
continue time without end.

While Man then possesses the external senses in common
with the lower animals, the specific nature of human
reason is notified in Judgment, Speech and Action. Reason
judges of good and bad, and in conformity with that
judgment the will is determined. But in particular the
significance which Language has for the soul's life of cognition is to be emphasised. A concept which cannot be denoted
by some expression in some language is not thinkable at
all. The word is the body of the thought, which cannot
exist absolutely *per se*.

But it is difficult to see how this understanding of the
relation between concept and expression is to square with
other opinions of the Brethren.

9. At its highest stage the teaching of the Brethren
becomes a Philosophy of Religion. Its purpose is a reconciliation between Science and Life, Philosophy and Faith.
Now in these matters men differ greatly. The ordinary
man requires a sensuous worship of God; but just as the
souls of animals and plants are beneath the soul of the
ordinary man, so above it are the souls of the philosopher
and the prophet with whom the pure angel is associated.
In the higher stages the soul is raised also above the lower
popular religion with its sensuous conceptions and usages.

No doubt Christianity and the Zoroastrian faith appeared

to the Brethren to be more perfect religious revelations.
'Our Prophet, Mohammed', they said, 'was sent to an unci-
vilized people, composed of dwellers in the desert, who
neither possessed a proper conception of the beauty of this
world, nor of the spiritual character of the world beyond.
The crude expressions of the Koran, which are adapted to
the understanding of that people, must be understood in
a spiritual sense by those who are more cultured'.

But the truth is not presented in its purity even in the
other national religions. There is a rational faith above
them all for which the Brethren moreover tried to find a
metaphysical derivation. Between God and his first creature,
the Creative Spirit, there is interposed by way of hypostasis
the Divine World-Law *(nâmûs)*. That World-Law extends
over everything, and is the wise arrangement of a merciful
Creator, who intends evil |to no one. Belief in a God of
Anger, in the punishment of Hell and the like, the Brethren declare to be irrational. Such a faith does harm to
the soul. The ignorant, sinful soul finds its hell even in
this life and in its own body. On the other hand, Resurrection is the separation of the soul from its body, and
the great Resurrection at the last day is the separation of
the Universal soul from the world, and its return to God.
This turning to God indeed is the aim in all religions.

10. The ethical system of the Brethren has an ascetic,
spiritualistic character, although here too their eclecticism
is shewn. According to it man is acting rightly, when he
follows his proper nature; 'praiseworthy is the free act of
the soul; admirable are the actions which have proceeded
from rational consideration; and lastly, obedience to the
Divine World-Law is worthy of the reward of being raised

to the celestial world of spheres. But this requires longing for what is above; and therefore the highest virtue is Love, which strives after union with God, the first loved one, and which is evinced even in this life in the form of religious patience and forbearance with all created beings. Such love gains in this life serenity of soul, freedom of heart and peace with the whole world, and in the life to come ascension to Eternal Light.'

After all this we need not wonder that the body was depreciated a good deal. 'Our true essence is the soul, and the highest aim of our existence should be to live, with Socrates, devoted to the Intellect, and with Christ, to the Law of Love. Nevertheless the body must be properly treated and looked after in order that the soul may have time to attain its full development.' In this view the Brethren set up an ideal type of human culture, whereof the features were borrowed from the characteristics of various nations. 'The ideal, and morally perfect man, should be of East-Persian derivation, Arabic in faith, of Irak, i. e. Babylonian, education, a Hebrew in astuteness, a disciple of Christ in conduct, as pious as a Syrian Monk, a Greek in the individual sciences, an Indian in the interpretation of all mysteries, but lastly and especially, a Sufi in his whole spiritual life.'

11. The attempt to establish in this way a reconciliation between knowledge and faith satisfied neither side. Theological dialecticians looked down upon the interpretation of the Koran given by the Brethren, just as the divines of our day look down upon the N. T. exegesis of Count Tolstoi. And the more rigid Aristotelians regarded the Pythagorean-Platonic tendency of the Encyclopaedia

much as a modern professor of philosophy is wont to look upon Spiritism, Occultism, and phenomena of that nature. But the writings, or at any rate the opinions, of the Faithful Brethren of Basra have exercised an important influence on the great body of the educated or half-educated world, — an influence to which eloquent attestation is borne by the very fact that so many manuscripts, mostly of recent date, are to be met with, of this extensive Encyclopaedia. Among many sects within the world of Islam, such as the Batinites, the Ismaelites, the Assasins, the Druses, or whatever may be their names, we find again the same doctrines in the main. In this form Greek wisdom has best succeeded in making itself at home in the East, while the Aristotelian School-Philosophy would only thrive, with few exceptions, in the hothouse-cultivation bestowed upon it at the courts of princely patrons. The great religious father, Gazali, is ready enough to toss aside the wisdom of the Brethren as mere popular philosophy, but he does not hesitate to take over what was good in them. He owes more to their body of ideas than he would perhaps have cared to avow. And their treatises have been turned to profit by others besides, particularly in Encyclopaediac works. The influence of the Encyclopaedia continues even yet in the Muslim East. In vain was it burned in Bagdad in the year 1150, along with the writings of Ibn Sina.

IV. THE NEO-PLATONIC ARISTOTELIANS OF THE EAST.

---

1. KINDI. [1]

1. Kindi is related in various ways to the Mutazilite Dialecticians and the Neo-Pythagorean Natural-Philosophers of his time, and we might therefore have dealt with him among the latter, even before Razi (v. III, 1, § 5). But yet tradition with one accord represents him as the first Peripatetic in Islam. What justification exists for this traditionary view will be seen in what follows, so far as an inference can be drawn from the few and imperfectly-preserved writings of this philosopher which have come down to us.

Abu Yaqub ibn Ishaq al-Kindi (*i. e.* of the tribe of Kinda) was of Arabian origin, and therefore was called the "Arabian" philosopher, to distinguish him from the numerous non-Arab associates of his, who had taken to the study of secular wisdom. He traced his genealogy to the old Kinda princes, although whether he was entitled to do so we need not seek to decide. The South-Arabian tribe of Kinda was

[1] Cf. my Article "On Kindi and his School" in Stein's 'Archiv für Geschichte der Philosophie XIII', p. 153 *sqq.*, from which I have taken over, without much alteration, not a little that appears in this chapter.

in any case farther advanced in outward civilization than other tribes. Many Kindite families too had for long been settlers in Iraq (Babylonia); and there, in the town of Kufa, of which his father was governor, our philosopher was born, probably in the beginning of the ninth century. He received his education, it would appear, partly in Basra, and thereafter in Bagdad, and therefore in the headquarters of the culture of his time. Here he came to put a higher value upon Persian civilization and Greek wisdom than upon old Arab virtue and the Muslim faith. He maintained even, — no doubt, following others —, that Kakhtan, the ancestor of the South-Arabians was a brother of Yaunan's, from whom the Greeks were descended. It was possible to make an observation of that kind in Bagdad at the Abbasid court, for there they knew of no nationality, and regarded the ancient Greeks with admiration.

It is not known how long Kindi remained at court, or what position he held there. He is mentioned as a translator of Greek works into Arabic, and is said to have revised and improved translations made by others, for example, in the case of the so-called "Theology of Aristotle". Numerous servants and disciples, whose names have been handed down to us, were probably set to this work under his supervision. Farther, he may have rendered services to the court in the capacity of astrologer or physician, and perhaps even in the administration of the revenues. But in later years he was dismissed, when he with others was made to suffer from the restoration of orthodoxy under Mutawakkil (847—861); and his library was for a long time confiscated. As regards personal character, tradition reproaches him with having been niggardly, — a stigma, however, which appears to have rested upon many other literary men and lovers of books.

The year of Kindi's death is as little known as that of his birth. He appears thus to have been out of court-favour when he died, or at least to have been in a subordinate position. It is strange that Masudi (v. II, 4 § 4), who had a great regard for him, is utterly silent on this point; but it seems in the highest degree probable from one of his astrological treatises that he was still alive subsequent to the year 870. The expiry of some petty astronomical cycle was imminent at that date, and this was being utilized by the Karmatites for the overthrow of the reigning family. In this matter, however, Kindi was loyal enough to make out the prolongation, for about 450 years, of the State's existence, menaced though it was by a planetary conjunction. His princely patron might well be satisfied; and history conformed to the time predicted, to within half-a-century. [1]

2. Kindi was a man of extraordinary erudition, a Polyhistor: he had absorbed the whole learning and culture of his time. But although he may have set down and communicated observations of his own as a geographer, a historian of civilization and a physician, he was in no respect a creative genius. His theological views bear a Mutazilite stamp. He wrote specially on Man's power of action, and the time of its appearance, i. e. whether it was before the act or whether it was synchronous with the act. The righteousness and the unity of God he expressly emphasized. In opposition

---

[1] [*Translator's note.* — The Bagdad Caliphate lasted up to the death of Mustassim (A. H. 656 or A. D. 1258), i. e. for 400 Mohammedan years after A. H. 256 or A. D. 870].

to the theory, — known at that time as Indian or Brahmanic, — that Reason is the sole and sufficient source of
knowledge, he defended prophecy, while yet he sought to
bring it into harmony with reason. His acquaintance with
various systems of religion impelled him to compare them
together, and he found as a common element in them all
the belief that the world was the work of a First Cause,
One and Eternal, for whom our knowledge furnishes us
with no more precise designation. It is however the duty
of the discerning to recognize this First Cause·as divine;
and God himself has shewn them the way thereto, and
has sent them ambassadors to bear witness for him, who
are instructed to promise everlasting bliss to the obedient,
and to threaten corresponding punishment to those who
do not obey.

3. Kindi's actual philosophy, like that of his contemporaries, consists, first and especially, of Mathematics and Natural
Philosophy, in which Neo-Platonism and Neo-Pythagoreanism
merge into one another. According to him no one can
be a philosopher without studying Mathematics. Fanciful
play upon letters and numbers is frequently met with in
his writings. Mathematics he also applied to Medicine in
his theory of the compound remedies. In fact he based the
efficacy of these remedies, like the effect of music, upon
geometrical proportion. It is here a matter of the propor-
tionality of the sensible qualities, warm, cold, dry and
moist. If a remedy has to be warm in the first degree,
it must possess double the warmth of the equable mixture,
— in the second degree, four times as much, and so on.
Kindi seems to have entrusted the decision of this point
to Sense, particularly to the sense of Taste, so that in him

we might have a hint of the proportional relation existing between stimulus and sensation. Yet that view, though quite original, was with him a mere piece of mathematical play. However, Cardan, a philosopher of the Renaissance, on the ground of this doctrine, reckoned him among the twelve most subtle-minded thinkers.

4. In Kindi's opinion, as has already been said, the world is a work of God, but His influence in its descent is transmitted through many intermediate agencies. All higher existence affects the lower, but that which is caused has no influence upon its cause, standing as this does above it in the scale of Being. In all the events of the world there is a pervading causality, which makes it possible for us, from our knowledge of the cause, to foretell the future, — for example, of the positions of the heavenly bodies. Farther, in any single existing thing, if it is thoroughly known, we possess a mirror, in which we may behold the entire scheme of things.

It is to the Spirit or Mind that the higher reality and all activity belong, and matter has to dispose itself in conformity with the desire of the Spirit. Midway between the Spirit of God and the material and bodily world stands the Soul, and it is the Soul which first called into being the world of the Spheres. From this Soul of the world the Human Soul is an emanation. In its nature, that is, in its operations, it is bound to the body with which it is united, but in its spiritual essence it is independent of the body; and thus the influences of the stars, which are limited to physical occurrences, do not affect it. Kindi goes on to say that our Soul is an uncompounded, imperishable substance, descended from the world of reason into that of the senses, but endowed with a recollection of its earlier condition. It does not feel at home here, for it has many needs, the satisfaction of which is denied to it, and which consequently are attended with painful emotions. Verily there is nothing constant in this world of coming and going, in which we may be deprived at any moment of what we love. Only in the world of reason is stability to be found. If then we desire to see our wishes fulfilled, and would not be deprived of what is dear to us, we must turn to the eternal blessings of reason, to the fear of God, to science, and to good works. But if we follow merely after material possessions in the belief that we can retain them, we are pursuing an object which does not really exist.

5. Kindi's theory of knowing corresponds to the ethical and metaphysical duality of the sensible and the spiritual. According to it our knowledge is either knowledge conveyed by the senses, or knowledge acquired by the reason: that which lies between, — the Fancy or Imagination, — is called a mediating faculty. The senses, then, apprehend the Particular, or the material Form, but the reason conceives the Universal, — species and genera, or the spiritual Form. And just as that which is perceived is one with Sense-Perception, so too that which is conceived by the reason is one with Reason itself.

Here then emerges for the first time the doctrine of the Reason or of the Spirit or Mind, (νοῦς, ʿaql) in a form in which, merely modified somewhat, it occupies a large space with the later Muslim philosophers. It continued to be a characteristic feature of philosophy in Islam throughout its whole course. And just as in the controversy regarding Universals in the Christian Middle Ages an objective and scientific interest is made evident also, so in the philosophical discussions of the Muslims concerning the thinking Spirit, the subjective requirement of intellectual culture is brought conspicuously to the front.

Kindi has a fourfold division of the Spirit [1]: first the Spirit which is ever real, — the Cause and the Essence of all that is spiritual in the world, — thus without doubt God or the First Spirit produced; second, Spirit as the Reasoning capacity or Potentiality of the human soul; third, as the Habit or actual possession of the soul, which it can make use of at any moment, just as, for example, the writer can make use of his art; fourth and last, as Activity, by which a reality within the soul may be carried over to the reality that is without. The Activity last named appears, according to Kindi, to be the act of Man himself, while to the First Cause, — to the ever-existing Spirit, — he ascribes the carrying of Potentiality into Habit, or the realisation of the Possible. The real Spirit or Mind we have thus received from above, and the third *'aql* is therefore called *'aql mustafad*, (Lat. *intellectus adeptus sive adquisitus*). The fundamental view of antiquity, — that all our knowledge about things must come from a source outside of us —, runs, in the form of this doctrine of the *'aql mustafad* or Spirit which we receive from above, through the whole of Arabian Philosophy, and thence passes into Christian Philosophy. Unfortunately the theory is nearly correct, as far as this philosophy is itself concerned, for the

---

[1] The Arabic *'aql* (νοῦς) is usually translated by Reason and Intelligence (Lat. *intellectus* and *intelligentia*). I prefer however the rendering, *Geist*, Spirit or Mind, because the expression includes God and the pure (separate) spirits of the spheres. Moreover it is hard to decide how far the personification of Reason was carried by individual thinkers.

'Active Spirit', which has created it, is in reality the Neo-Platonic Aristotle.

Man has always attributed to his God or Gods the highest of his own possessions. Muslim theologians directly attribute to the divine agency the moral actions of men. But in the opinion of the philosophers, Knowing is of more importance than Doing. The latter, having more to do with the lower world of the senses, may possibly be Man's own; but his highest knowledge, the pure Reason, comes from above, — from the Divine Essence.

It is clear that the doctrine of the Spirit, as it stands in Kindi, goes back to the 'Nous'-doctrine of Alexander of Aphrodisias in his second book "On the Soul". But Alexander expressly maintained that according to Aristotle there is a threefold 'Nous'. Kindi says on the contrary that he is representing the opinion of Plato and Aristotle. In this the Neo-Pythagorean and the Neo-Platonic views unite: for in everything the number 'Four' must be pointed out, and Plato and Aristotle brought into agreement.

6. Let us now sum up: Kindi is a Mutazilite theologian and Neo-Platonic philosopher with Neo-Pythagorean additions. Socrates, the martyr of Athenian heathenism, is his ideal: on him, his fate and his teaching he has composed several works; and he seeks to combine Plato and Aristotle in Neo-Platonic fashion.

Tradition nevertheless calls him the first who followed Aristotle in his writings; and assuredly this representation is not altogether unfounded. In the long list of his works Aristotle takes a prominent place. He was not satisfied with merely translating him, but he studied his translated works and endeavoured to improve and explain them. At

all events the Aristotelian Physics, with the commentary
of Alexander of Aphrodisias, had an important influence
upon him. Such assertions as that the world is only potentially unending and not actually so, and that motion is
continuous, and the like, point rather in that direction.
The Natural-Philosophers of that day, as well as the Faithful
Brethren, said for instance, that motion had as little con-
tinuity as number. But farther, Kindi resolutely turned
away from the marvel-mongering philosophy of the time,
by declaring Alchemy an imposture. That which nature
alone could produce, he held to be beyond the power of
man. Whoever then gives himself up to alchemistic experiments, is in his opinion deceiving either himself or others.
The famous physician, Razi, attempted to controvert this
view of Kindi's.

7. The influence of Kindi as a teacher and an author
has operated mainly through his Mathematics, Astrology,
Geography and Medicine. His most faithful and certainly
his most notable disciple was Akhmed ibn Mohammed
al-Tayyib al-Sarakhsi († 899), a government official and friend
of the Caliph Mutadid, to whose negligence or caprice he
fell a victim. He worked at Alchemy and Astrology, strove
to gain a knowledge of the wisdom and might of the
Creator from the wonders of creation, and prosecuted
the study of Geography and History. Another disciple of
Kindi's has become better known, — Abu Mashar († 885),
who, however, owes all his reputation to Astrology. He is
said to have become, when 47 years of age, an admirer of
Kindi's, — though up till then he had been a fanatical
opponent of philosophy, — having been attracted to the
pursuit of Astrology, by a superficial study of Mathematics.

Whether this be truth or fiction, such a course of education is at all events characteristic of that inquisitive grasping at half-understood knowledge, which peculiarly belongs to the first centuries of Arab Science.

The school of Kindi went in no way beyond the master. Of its literary activity hardly any sample has been preserved to us beyond a stray quotation or two. It is of course possible that in the treatises of the Faithful Brethren, something of it may have been saved, but this cannot be determined, in the present state of our knowledge.

2. FARABI.

1. In the tenth century the Logicians or Metaphysicians are distinguished from the Natural-Philosophers. The former follow a more rigorous method than the Dialecticians, and treat of other subjects than those which are dealt with by the Physical school. They have repudiated Pythagoras, to entrust themselves to the guidance of Aristotle, of course in Neo-Platonic guise.

We have here to do with two directions of scientific interest. The Natural-Philosophers are more or less concerned with the plenitude of the concrete phenomena of Nature, as in Geography and Ethnology. They investigate in all directions the effects of things, and think the essential nature of these is only to be discerned in such effect or working. When they do ascend beyond Nature, Soul and Spirit, to the Divine Essence, then the definition of it to which they confine themselves, or which they adopt by preference, is — 'the First Cause', or, — 'the wise Creator', whose goodness and wisdom appear from his works.

The Logicians proceed in a very different way. The occurrence of the Particular has only a subordinate value in their eyes, — the value, merely, of an illustration of its deducibility from the Universal. While the Physicists start from effects or operations, the Logicians seek to comprehend things from principles. Everywhere they enquire after the Idea or Essence of things, up to the highest. For them, — to make the contrast more intelligible by an example —, God is not, first of all, 'the wise Creator', but first of all 'the necessarily existing Being'.

In the order of time the Logicians come after the Physical school, just as the Mutazilite Dialectic on its part (v. II, 3 §§ 4 and 5) brought within the scope of its consideration first God's Working, and then his Being.

We have already come to recognize Razi as the most important representative of the philosophical direction taken by the Physicists; and as for the Logical and Metaphysical efforts, — for which Kindi and others had prepared the way, — they culminate with Razi's younger contemporary Abu Nasr ibn Mohammed ibn Tarkhan ibn Uzlag al-Farabi.

2. We cannot say much with certainty about the course of Farabi's outward life and training. He was a quiet man, devoted to a life of philosophy and contemplation, sheltered by the powerful, and assuming at last the dress of a Sufi. His father is said to have been a Persian general, and he himself was born at Wasidj, a small fortified place in the district of Farab in Turkish Transoxiana. It was in Bagdad, and partly at the hands of a Christian preceptor Yohanna ibn Hailan, that he received his education. This embraced both literary and mathematical subjects, forming the equivalent of the 'Trivium' and 'Quadrivium' of mediæval

Christendom. One or two of his writings, particularly on Music, give evidence still of his mathematical training. Legend credits him with ability to speak in all the languages of the world, seventy in number. That he understood Turkish and Persian, — an *a priori* probability, — is manifest from his works. Arabic he writes clearly, and with a certain grace, although now and then his fondness for synonyms and parallel clauses interferes with the precision of philosophical expression.

The philosophy in which Farabi was initiated sprung from the school of Merv; and perhaps its members had given greater attention to metaphysical questions than the men of Harran and Basra with their marked leaning to Natural Philosophy.

From Bagdad, where he had long lived and worked, he went to Haleb (Aleppo), in consequence doubtless of political disturbances, and there he settled at the brilliant court of Saif-addaula; but he must have spent his closing years not at court but in retirement. He died at Damascus, while on a journey, in December, 950; and it is reported that his prince, attired as a Sufi, pronounced over him his funeral oration. We are told that he was eighty years of age, and it is otherwise probable that he was a very old man. His contemporary, and partner in study, Abu Bishr Matta died ten years before him, and his pupil Abu Zakariya Yakhya ibn Adi in the year 971, at the age of eighty-one.

3. The chronological order of the works of Farabi has not been determined. Shorter treatises in which he comes into touch with the Dialecticians and Natural-Philosophers, if these are at all genuine in the form handed down to us, may have been popular or juvenile productions of his;

but his mature powers were applied to the study of Aristotle's writings, for which reason the name given him by the East was 'the Second Teacher', that is, 'the Second Aristotle'.

Since his day the number and order of the works composed by Aristotle or at least attributed to him, which have been paraphrased and commented on after Farabi's example, remain upon the whole fixed. First come the eight Logical treatises, viz., the Categories; the Hermeneutics; the First Analytics; the Second Analytics; the Topics; the Sophistics; Rhetoric; and the Poetics: It is to these that the Isagoge of Porphyry is the introduction. Then follow the eight treatises which deal with Physical subjects, *viz.*, Auscultatio Physica; De Coelo et Mundo; De Generatione et Corruptione; the Meteorology; the Psychology; De Sensu et Sensato; the Book of Plants; and the Book of Animals. Lastly come the Metaphysics, the Ethics, the Politics and so on.

The so-called "Theology of Aristotle" was still considered by Farabi to be a genuine work. In Neo-Platonic fashion, and with some attempt at adaptation to the Muslim faith, he seeks to demonstrate that Plato and Aristotle harmonize with one another. The need which he experiences is not for a discriminating criticism, but for a conclusive and comprehensive view of the world; and the satisfaction of this need, — which is rather a religious than a scientific one, — induces him to overlook philosophic differences. Plato and Aristotle must differ from each other only in method, in phraseology, and in relation to practical life: their doctrine of wisdom is the same. They are the 'Imāms' or 'highest authorities' in philosophy; and seeing that they were two, independent, original minds, the authority which is constituted by their agreement has more validity in the eyes of Farabi than the faith of the whole Muslim community, who with blind confidence follow the guidance of one.

4. Farabi is counted among the physicians, but he seems not to have been in actual practice. He was entirely devoted to the spiritual healing art. Purity of Soul he denominated the condition and fruit of all philosophizing, and he demanded love of truth even though it should oppose Aristotle. Then the judgment has to be trained by means of Geometry and Logic for the study of physical and mental science. Farabi, however, pays but little heed to the separate branches of study: his powers are concentrated on Logic, Metaphysics, and the principles of Physics. Philosophy for him is the science of all Being as such, in the acquisition of which science we come to resemble the Godhead. It is the one, all-embracing science, which pictures the world to us as a Universe. Farabi's charge against the Dialecticians is, that they employ as a basis for their demonstrations the deliverances of ordinary consciousness without testing them; and the Natural-Philosophers he blames for continually occupying themselves merely with the effect of things, and thus never getting beyond the contrasts of worldly phenomena by attaining to a unified conception of the All. He would confront the former by setting Thought on a proper foundation; and in opposition to the latter he would thoroughly investigate the subject of the One First Cause of all that exists. Consequently we shall be taking the best way to do justice to his historical and dogmatic position, if we endeavour to give some account, first of his Logic, next of his Metaphysics, and finally of his Physics and Practical Philosophy.

5. The Logic of Farabi is not a mere analysis of scientific thinking: it contains in addition many remarks on grammar, and discussions on the theory of knowledge. While grammar is limited to the language of one people, Logic, on the other hand, has to regulate the expression in language of the aggregate intelligence of mankind. From the simplest elements of speech it must advance to the most complex forms, — from the word to the sentence, and on to discourse.

Logic falls into two divisions, according as its subjects stand related to actuality; the first of these comprising the doctrine of Ideas and Definitions (*tasawwur*), and the second, the doctrine of Judgments, Inferences, and Proofs (*tasdiq*). Ideas, — with which are classed Definitions, though in a mere loose, outward juxtaposition, — have in themselves no relation to actuality, that is to say, they are neither true nor false. Among 'Ideas' Farabi recognizes here the simplest psychological forms, that is, both the representations of individual objects arising from Sense-Perception, and those ideas which have been stamped upon the mind from the first, such as the Necessary, the Actual, the Possible. Such representations and ideas are immediately certain. A man's mind may be directed to these, and his soul made observant of them, but they cannot be demonstrated to him, nor can they be explained by deriving them from what is known, seeing that they are already clear in themselves, and that too with the highest degree of certitude.

By combining representations or ideas, judgments result, and these may be either true or false. To obtain a foundation for these judgments we have to go back through the processes of Inference and of Proof to certain propositions originally conveyed to the understanding, immediately obvious, and admitting of no farther confirmation. Such propositions, — the fundamental propositions or Axioms of all Science, — there must be for Mathematics, Metaphysics, and Ethics.

The doctrine of Proof, by which, starting from what is known and well-established, we arrive at a knowledge of something formerly unknown, is, according to Farabi, Logic properly so called. Acquaintance with the leading Concepts (the Categories), and with their synthesis in Judgment (Hermeneutics) and in Inference (First Analytics) furnishes only the introduction thereto. And in the Proof-doctrine the chief point is to ascertain the Norms or principles of a universally valid and necessary Science, which Philosophy has to be. Here the Law of Contradiction is looked upon as the highest of these principles, by which law the truth or necessity of a proposition, and at the same time the untruth or impossibility of the contrary, become known in one single cognitive act. From this point of view the Platonic Dichotomy is to be preferred, as a scientific method, to the Aristotelian Polytomy. And Farabi is not content with the formal side of the doctrine of proof. That doctrine has to be more than a methodology which points out the right way to the truth: it must itself point out the truth; it must generate science. It not only deals with judgments as material for the syllogism, but it enquires also into the truth which they contain, with reference to the particular sciences concerned. It is not a mere implement; it is rather a constituent part of philosophy.

As we have seen, the theory of proof terminates in necessary knowledge, corresponding to necessary existence. But besides this there is the great province of the Possible, from which we can gain only a probable knowledge. The different degrees then of probability, or the modes in which we attain to a knowledge of the Possible, are discussed in the Topics, and with them are associated Sophistic, Rhetoric and Poetics. In other connections these last three subjects are mainly concerned with practical aims, but in Farabi's hands they are combined with the Topics into a Dialectic of the Seeming. He proceeds to say that true science can be built up only on the necessary propositions of the Second Analytics, but that Probability shades off into the mere phantom of truth, from the topical or dialectic judgments down to the poetical. Thus Poetry stands at the very bottom of the scale, being in Farabi's opinion a lying and immoral absurdity.

In the addendum to the Isagoge of Porphyry, our philosopher has also given expression to his views on the question of 'Universals'. He finds the Particular not only in things and in sense-perception but also in thought. In like manner the Universal exists not merely as an 'accident' in individual things, but also as a 'substance' in mind. The mind of man abstracts the Universal from things, but it had an existence of its own before these. Virtually therefore the triple distinction of the *ante rem*, *in re* and *post rem* already occurs in Farabi.

Does mere 'being' also belong to the Universals? Is existence, in effect, a predicate? This question which caused so much mischief in philosophy was fully and correctly answered by Farabi. According to him, existence is a grammatical or logical relation, but not a category of actuality which makes any assertion about things. The existence of a thing is nothing but the thing itself.

6. The trend of thought found in the Logic asserts itself also in the Metaphysics. Instead of the Changeable and the Everlasting, there emerge the ideas of the Possible. and the Necessary.

Everything in fact that exists, is, in Farabi's view, either a necessary or a possible thing; there is no third kind of Being. Now since all which is possible presupposes for its realisation a Cause, while yet the chain of causes cannot be traced back without end, we see ourselves compelled to assume that there is a Being, existing of necessity, uncaused, possessing the highest degree of perfection and an eternal plenitude of reality, self-sufficing, without any change, who as absolute Mind and pure goodness and thinking, — being the thinking and the thought in one nature, — loves the all-transcending goodness and beauty of that nature, which is his own. This Being cannot be proved to exist, because he himself is the proof and first cause of all things, in whom truth and reality coincide. And it is involved in the very idea of such a Being, that he should be one, and one only, for if there were two first and absolute Beings, they would have to be partly alike and partly different, — in which case, however, the simplicity of each would be destroyed. A Being who is the most perfect of all, must be one alone.

This first Existence, one alone, and of a verity real, we call God; and since in him all things are one, without even difference in kind, no definition of his Being can be supplied. Yet man bestows upon him the noblest names, expressive of all that is most honoured and esteemed in life, because in the mystic impulse thereto, words lose their usual significance, transcending all discrepancy. Some names refer to his essential nature, others to his relation to the world, without prejudicing, however, the unity of his essence; but they are all to be understood metaphorically, and we can interpret them only according to feeble analogy. Of God, as the most perfect Being, we ought properly to have also the most complete idea. At least our mathematical notions are more perfect than our notions of physics, because the former refer to the more perfect objects. But with the most perfect object of all we fare as with the most brilliant light: by reason of the weakness of our eyes we cannot bear it. Thus the imperfections inherent in Matter cling to our understanding.

7. We are able to see God better in the regular gradation of Beings which proceed from him than in himself. From him, the One alone, comes the All, for his knowledge is the highest power: In his cognizance of himself the world comes into being: The cause of all things is not the will of an almighty Creator, but the knowledge of the Necessary. From eternity the Forms or Types of things are in God, and from him eternally proceeds also his own image, termed 'the Second All' or 'the first created Spirit', which moves the outermost celestial Sphere. In succession to this Spirit, come, one out of the other, the eight Spirits of the Spheres, all of which are unique in their several kinds and perfect, and these are the creators of the celestial bodies. These nine Spirits, called 'Celestial Angels', together form the second grade of Being. In the third grade stands the Reason, active in Humanity, which is also termed the Holy Spirit and which unites heaven and earth. The Soul is in the fourth grade. These two, the Reason and the Soul, do not remain by themselves in their strict original

One-ness, but multiply in accordance with the great number of human beings. Lastly appear Form and Matter, as Beings of the fifth and sixth orders; and with them the series of Spiritual existences is closed. The first three grades, God, the Spirits of the Spheres, and the Active Reason, remain Spirit *per se*; but the three which follow, — Soul, Form and Matter, although incorporeal, yet enter into relation with Body.

The Corporeal, which is held to originate in the imagination of the Spirit, has also its six grades: Celestial Bodies, Human Bodies, Bodies of Lower Animals, Bodies of Plants, Minerals, and Elementary Bodies.

The influence of Farabi's Christian preceptor is probably still to be seen in these speculations, following as they do the number Three. That number had the same significance in them that the number Four had with the Natural-Philosophers. The terminology also bears out this idea.

That, however, is merely external: It is Neo-Platonism that contributes the contents. Here the Creation, or Emanation of the world, appears as an eternal, intellectual process. By the first created Spirit thinking of its Author, the second Sphere-spirit comes into being; while, by the same Spirit thinking of itself and thus realizing itself, there proceeds from it the first Body, or the uppermost celestial Sphere. And so the process goes on in necessary succession, down to the lowest Sphere, that of the Moon, in entire accordance with the Ptolemaic Sphere-system, — as it is known to every well-educated person at least from Dante's "Commedia", — and in the Neo-Platonic manner of derivation. The Spheres together form an unbroken order, for all that exists is a Unity. The creation and preservation of the

world are one and the same. And not only is the unity
of the Divine Being portrayed in the world, but the Divine
righteousness is also expressed in the beautiful order which
there prevails. The logical order of the world is at the
same time a moral order.

8. The sublunary world of this earth is, of course, wholly
dependent on the world of the celestial spheres. Yet the
influence from above bears in the first place, as we know
a priori, upon the necessary order of the whole, although
in the second place the individual thing also is made to
happen, but only according to natural reciprocal action,
and therefore by rules which experience teaches us. Astrology,
which attributes everything that is contingent or extraordinary to the stars and their conjunctions, is combated
by Farabi. There is no certain knowledge of the Contingent; and, — as Aristotle also has taught, — much of
what happens on this earth possesses in a high degree the
character of the Contingent or the Possible. The celestial
world, on the other hand, has another and a more perfect
nature, which operates according to necessary laws. It can
bestow upon this earthly world only that which is good;
and therefore it is a complete mistake to maintain that
some stars bring good luck, and others ill luck. The nature
of the heavens is one, and it is uniformly good. The conclusion then at which Farabi arrives, by these reflections
is this: Knowledge, capable of demonstration, and perfectly
certain, is afforded by Mathematical Astronomy alone; the
physical study of the heavens yields a probable knowledge;
but the tenets and vaticinations of Astrology merit an
exceedingly hesitating belief.

Overagainst the simplicity of the celestial world we have

the sublunary kingdom of the four natures, — the kingdom of contrasts and of change. Even in this realm, in the midst of its plurality, we meet with the unity of an ascending series, from the Elements up to Man. Farabi is unable to advance much that is original on this subject. True to his logical standpoint, he gives himself very little concern about the Natural Sciences, among which, in reliance upon the original unity of matter, he seems without any hesitation to have counted Alchemy. We turn at once to his Doctrine of Man or of the Human Soul, which presents a measure of interest.

9. The powers or divisions of the Human Soul are, in Farabi's opinion, not of co-ordinate rank, but constitute an ascending series. The lower faculty is Material for the higher; and this again is the Form for the first, while the highest power of all, viz. Thinking, is non-material, and is Form for all the Forms which precede. The life of the Soul is raised from things of sense to thought, by means of the power of Representation; but in all the faculties there is involved Effort or Will. Every theory has its obverse side in practice; and Inclination and Disinclination are inseparable from the perceptions furnished by the senses. To the representations of these the soul takes up an attitude of assent or dissent, by affirming or denying. Finally, Thought passes judgment on Good and Bad, gives to the Will its motives, and constructs Art and Science. All Perception, Representation or Thought is attended with a certain effort to reach the necessary consequence, just as warmth radiates from the substance of fire.

The Soul is that which gives completeness (Entelechia) to the existence of the body; but that which gives completeness to the existence of the Soul is the Mind, or the Spirit (*'aql*). The Spirit only is the real Man.

10. Accordingly the discusion turns mainly on the Mind or Spirit. In the human Spirit everything earthly is raised to a higher mode of existence, which is lifted out of the categories of the Corporeal. Now as a capability or potentiality, Mind or Spirit is present in the Soul of the Child; and it becomes actual Spirit in the course of its apprehension of bodily forms in experience by means of the Senses and the representative faculty. But this transition from possibility to actuality, — the realisation thus of experience, — is not Man's own act, but is brought about by the Superhuman Spirit, which has sprung from the last Sphere-Spirit, that of the Moon. In this way Man's knowledge is represented as being a contribution from above, and not a knowledge which has been acquired in mental struggle. In the light of the Spirit which stands above us, our understanding descries the Forms of the Corporeal; and thereby experience is amplified into rational knowledge. Experience, in fact, takes in only the Forms which have been abstracted from the world of Matter. But there are in existence also, — before and above material things, — Forms and general entities, in the pure Spirits of the Spheres. Man now receives information from these 'detached Forms': it is only by means of their influence that his actual experience becomes explicable to him. From God down to the Spirit of Mankind, the higher Form affects only that which immediately succeeds it. Every intermediate Form stands in a relation of 'receptive' activity to what is above it, and of 'conferring' activity to what is below it. In its relation to the Human Spirit, which is influenced from above (*'aql mustafad*),

the Superhuman Spirit, produced from the last Sphere-Spirit, is to be called 'active' or 'creative' (*'aql fa"âl*). Yet it is not continually active, because its effectiveness is restrained by its material. But God is the completely-real, eternally-active Spirit.

The Spirit in Man is threefold: according as it is (1) Possible, (2) Actual, and (3) Influenced from above. Now in the sense of Farabi, this means — that (1) the spiritual potentiality in Man is, by means of (2) realizing the knowledge which is gained by experience, (3) led to the knowledge of the Supersensible, which precedes all experience, and itself induces the experience.

The grades of Spirit and its knowledge correspond to the grades of existence. The lower strives wistfully to reach the higher, and the higher lifts the lower up to its own level. The Spirit which stands above us, and which has lent to all earthly things their Forms, seeks to bring these scattered Forms together that they may become one in love. First of all he collects them in Man. And indeed the possibility and truth of human knowledge depend on the fact that the same Spirit who bestowed upon the Corporeal its figure, also gives Idea to Man. The scattered Forms of the earthly are found again in the Human Spirit, and thereby it comes to resemble the last of the Celestial Spirits. Unity with that Celestial Spirit, — and in this an approach to God, — is the aim and the blessedness of the Spirit of Man.

Now the question whether such a union is possible before Man's death is, in Farabi's opinion, either a doubtful one, or one which should be answered in the direct negative. The highest thing that can be attained in this life, is

rational knowledge. But separation from the body gives
to the rational soul the complete freedom which belongs
to spirit. But does it then continue to exist as an individual
soul? Or is it merely a Moment of the higher World-
Intelligence? On this point Farabi expresses himself ambigu-
ously, and with a lack of consistency, in his various writings.
Men, — so the expression runs, — disappear in death;
one generation follows another; and like is joined to like,
each in its own class. And forasmuch as rational souls are
not bound to space, they multiply without end, just as
thought is added to thought, and power to power. Every
soul reflects on itself and all others that are like to it;
and the more it so reflects, the more intense is its joy
(Cf. *infra*, § 13).

11. We come now to Farabi's practical philosophy. In
his Ethics and Politics we are brought into a somewhat
closer relation to the life and belief of the Muslims. One
or two general points of view may be brought forward.

Just as Logic has to give an account of the principles
of knowledge, so Ethics have to deal with the fundamental
rules of conduct, although, in the latter, somewhat more
value is attached to practice and experience than in the
theory of knowledge. In the treatment of this subject
Farabi agrees sometimes with Plato, and sometimes with
Aristotle; but occasionally, in a mystic and ascetic fashion,
he goes farther than either of them. In opposition to the
Theologians, who recognize, no doubt, a knowledge gained
by Reason, but not rules of conduct taught by Reason, Farabi
frequently affirms with emphasis that Reason decides whether
a thing is good or evil. Why should not that Reason, which
has been imparted to us from above, decide upon conduct,

seeing that the highest virtue certainly consists in knowing? In vigorously accentuated terms Farabi declares that if one man knew everything that stands in the writings of Aristotle, but did not act in accordance with his knowledge, while another man shaped his conduct in accordance with Aristotle's teaching, without being acquainted with it, the preference would have to be assigned to the former. Knowledge takes a higher position than the moral act; otherwise it could not decide upon the act.

By its very nature the Soul desires. In so far as it perceives and represents, it has a will, just like the lower animals. But man alone possesses freedom of choice, seeing that this rests upon rational consideration. Pure thought is the sphere of freedom. Thus it is a freedom which depends upon motives furnished by thinking, — a freedom which is at the same time necessity, inasmuch as in the last resort it is determined by the rational nature of God. In this sense Farabi is a Determinist.

On account of the opposition offered by matter, the freedom of man, as thus conceived, can only imperfectly vindicate its lordship over the Sensible. It does not become perfect till the rational soul has been enfranchised from the bonds of matter and the wrappings of error, — in the life of the Spirit. But that is the highest blessedness which is striven after for its own sake, and consequently it is plainly the Good. Such good the Human Soul is seeking, when it turns to the Spirit above it, just as the Spirits of the heavens do, when they draw near to the Highest.

12. Even in the Ethics little regard is had to actual moral conditions; but in his Politics Farabi withdraws still farther from real life. In his oriental way of looking

at things, the ideal Republic of Plato merges into 'the Philosopher as Ruler'. Men, having been brought together by a natural want, submit themselves to the will of a single person, in whom the State, be it good or bad, is, so to speak, embodied. A State therefore is bad, if the head of it is, as regards the principles of the Good, either ignorant or in error, or quite depraved. On the other hand the good or excellent State has only one type, that namely in which the philosopher is ruler. And Farabi endows his 'Prince' with all the virtues of humanity and philosophy: he is Plato in the mantle of the Prophet Mohammed.

In the description of rulers representative of the ideal Prince, — for there may be more than one existing together, and Prince and minister may divide governing-virtue and wisdom between them, — we come nearer the Muslim political theory of that day. But the expressions are wrapped in obscurity: the lineage, for example, which is proper for a Prince, and his duty of taking the lead in the holy war, — are not clearly signified. All indeed is left floating in philosophic mist.

13. Morality reaches perfection only in a State which at the same time forms a religious community. Not only does the condition of the State determine the temporal lot of its citizens, but also their future destiny. The souls of citizens in an "ignorant" State are devoid of reason, and return to the elements as sensible Forms, in order to be united anew with other beings, — men or lower animals. In States which are "in error", and in those which are "depraved", the leader alone is responsible, and punishment awaits him in the world beyond; but the souls which have been led into error share the fate of the ignorant. On the

other hand, if the good and 'knowing' souls only maintain their ground, they enter the world of pure Spirit; and the higher the stage of knowledge to which they have attained in this life, the higher will their position be after death, in the order of the All, and the more intense their blessed delight.

In all likelihood expressions of this kind are only the outer wrapping of a mystico-philosophical belief in the absorption of the Human Spirit into the World-Spirit and finally into God. For, — as Farabi teaches, — although the world, deductively considered (*i. e.* logically and metaphysically), is something different from God, yet inductively the present world is regarded by the soul as being identical with the next, because in everything, even in his Unity, God is himself the All.

14. If we now take a general survey of Farabi's system, it exhibits itself as a fairly consistent Spiritualism, or, — to be more precise, — Intellectualism. The Corporeal, — that which appeals to the Senses, — as it orginates in the imagination of the Spirit, might be designated "a confused presentation". The only true existence is Spirit, although it assumes various degrees. God alone is entirely unmixed and pure Spirit, while those Spirits, which eternally proceed from him, already have in them the element of plurality. The number of primary Spirits has been determined by the Ptolemaic cosmology, and corresponds to the celestial hierarchy. The farther any one of them is removed from the first, so much the less part has it in the Being of the pure Spirit. From the last World-Spirit Man receives his essential nature, that is — Reason. There is no gap in all the system; the Universe is a beautiful and well-

ordered whole. The Evil and the Bad are the necessary consequence of finiteness in individual things; but the Good which characterizes the Universe is set thereby in bolder relief.

Can this fair order of the Universe, from all eternity emanating from God, ever be destroyed, or can it even flow back to God? A sustained streaming-back to the Godhead, there doubtless is. The longing of the Soul is directed to what is above; and advancing knowledge purifies it and leads it upwards. But how far? Neither philosophers nor prophets have been able to return a clear answer to this question. And the wisdom of both of these, — both philosophy and prophecy, — Farabi derives from the creative World-Spirit above us. Now and again he speaks of prophecy as if it represented the highest stage of human knowledge and action. But that cannot be his real view; — at least it is not the logical consequence of his theoretical philosophy. According to it everything prophetic, — in dream, vision, revelation and so on, — belongs to the sphere of the Imagination or Representation, and thus takes an intermediate position between Sense-Perception and pure Rational Knowledge. Although, in his Ethics and Politics, he attaches a high educational importance to religion, it is always regarded as inferior in absolute worth to knowledge acquired through pure reason.

Farabi lived perpetually in the world of the Intellect. A king in the mental realm, a beggar in worldly possessions, he felt happy with his books, and with the birds and flowers of his garden. To his people, — the Muslim community, — he could be only very little. In his political and ethical teaching there was no proper place for worldly matters or for the 'holy war'. His philosophy did not satisfy any need appertaining to the senses, while it spoke against the life of imagination belonging both to the senses and the intellect, as that life gives special expression to itself in the creations of Art and in religious fancies. He was lost in the abstractions of pure Spirit. As a pious, holy man, he was an object of wonder to his contemporaries, and by a few disciples he was honoured as the personification of wisdom; but by the genuine scholars of Islam he was always decried as a heretic. There was, of course, ground enough for this: just as Natural Philosophy easily led to Naturalism and Atheism, the Monotheism of the Logicians imperceptibly conducted to Pantheism.

15. Farabi had no great following of disciples: Abu Zakariya Yakhya ibn Adi, a Jacobite Christian, became known as a translator of Aristotelian works; but a pupil of Zakariya's came to be more spoken of, called Abu Sulaiman Mohammed ibn Tahir ibn Bahram al-Sidjistani, who gathered about him in Bagdad, in the second half of the tenth century, the learned men of his time. The conversational discussions which they conducted, and the philosophical instructions which were imparted by the master, have been to some extent preserved, and we can clearly see the outcome of the school. Just as Natural Philosophy drifted into a secret lore, and the school of Kindi abandoned Philosophy for the separate branches of Mathematical and Physical Science, so the logical tendency of Farabi passed into a philosophy of words. Distinctions and definitions form the subject of these conferences. Individual points in the history of philosophy and in the several sciences are discussed also, without any systematic connection; but almost never does any positive interest in these subjects

appear. The Human Soul occupies the foreground entirely, just as in the case of the Faithful Brethren, except that these last dealt rather with the marvellous operations of the Soul, while the Logicians pondered over its rational essence and its elevation to the Supra-rational. The Sidjistani Society trifled with words and concepts, instead of with numbers and letters after the fashion of the Brethren; but the end in both cases was — a mystical Sufism.

It is therefore no matter of astonishment that in the learned meetings of Abu Sulaiman, as reported by his pupil Tauhidi († 1009), Empedocles, Socrates, Plato and others are oftener mentioned than Aristotle. A very miscellaneous society came together in those meetings. No question was asked as to the country from which any one came, or the religion to which he adhered. They lived in the conviction, — derived from Plato, that every opinion contained a measure of truth, just as all things shared in a common existence, and all sciences in an actual knowledge which was one and the same. On that assumption alone could they have conceived that every one might start with maintaining that his own opinion was the true one, and that the science which he cultivated was the science most to be preferred. And for that very reason there is no conflict between Religion and Philosophy, however vehement the assertions may be on these two sides. On the contrary Philosophy confirms the doctrines of Religion, just as the latter brings the results of Philosophy to perfection. If Philosophical Knowledge is the essence and end of the Soul of man, Religious Belief is its life, or the way to that end; and as Reason is God's vicegerent on earth, it is impossible for Reason and Revelation to contradict each other.

It is not worth while to accentuate particular points in these conversational discussions, the tenor of which we have given. The appearance of Sidjistani and his circle is important in the history of culture; but it has no significance as regards the development of Philosophy in Islam. What was to Farabi the very life of his Spirit, becomes in this Society a subject merely of clever conversation.

3. IBN MASKAWAIH.

1. We have arrived at the point of time when the tenth century is passing into the eleventh. Farabi's school has apparently died out; and Ibn Sina, — destined to awaken into fresh life the philosophy of his predecessor, — is still a youth. Here however we have to make mention of a man, more allied, it is true, to Kindi than to Farabi, but who yet agrees with the latter in essential points, by reason of employing the same sources with him. He affords an instance also of the fact that the most sagacious minds of his time were not disposed to follow Farabi into the region of Logico-Metaphysical speculation.

This man is Abu Ali ibn Maskawaih, physician, philologist and historian, who was the treasurer and friend of the Sultan Adudaddaula, and who died full of years in 1030. Amongst other things he has left us a philosophical system of Ethics which up to this day is valued in the East. It is a combination of material taken from Plato, Aristotle, Galen and the Muslim Religious Law, although Aristotle predominates in it. It commences with a treatise on the Essential Nature of the Soul.

2. The Soul of Man, as Ibn Maskawaih explains, is a

simple, incorporeal substance, conscious of its own existence, knowledge and working. That it must be of a spiritual nature — follows from the very fact that it appropriates at one and the same time Forms the most opposed to each other, for example, the notions of white and black, while a body can only take up one of the two forms at a time. Farther, it apprehends both the forms of the Sensible and those of the Spiritual in the same spiritual manner, for Length is not 'long' in the soul, nor does it become 'longer' in the memory. Accordingly the knowledge and endeavour of the soul extend far beyond its own body: even the entire world of sense cannot satisfy it. Moreover it possesses an inborn rational knowledge, which cannot have been bestowed by the Senses, for it is by means of this knowledge that it determines the True and the False, in the course of comparing and distinguishing between the objects presented to it in Sense-Perception, — thus supervising and regulating the Senses. Finally, it is in Self-Consciousness, or knowing of its own knowing, that the spiritual unity of the soul is most clearly shewn, — a unity, in which thinking, that which thinks, and that which is thought — all coincide.

The human soul is distinguished from the souls of the lower animals particularly by rational reflection as the principle of its conduct, directed towards the Good.

3. That by which a Being, possessed of will, attains the end or the perfection of his nature is, in general terms, 'good'. A certain capability, therefore, or disposition, directed to an end is requisite, in order to be good. But as regards their capability men differ very essentially. Only a few, — Maskawaih thinks, — are by nature good, and

never become bad, since what is by nature, does not
change; while on the other hand, many are by nature bad,
and never become good. Others, however, who at first are
neither good nor bad, are definitely turned either in the
one direction or the other, through upbringing and social
intercourse.

Now the Good is either a general good or a particular
good. There is an absolute Good, which is identical with
the highest Being and the highest knowledge; and all the
good together strive to attain to it. But for every individual person a particular Good presents itself subjectively
under the aspect of Happiness or Pleasure; and this consists in the full and active manifestation of his own essential
nature, — in the complete realisation of his inmost being.

Speaking generally, — Man is good and happy, if he
acts as Man: Virtue is human excellence. But since humanity is presented as occupying different levels in different
individuals, Happiness or the Good is not the same for all.
And because an individual man, if he were left to his own
resources could not realize all the good things that might
otherwise be obtained, it is necessary that many should
live together. As a consequence of this condition, the first
of duties, or the foundation of all the virtues, is a general
love for humankind, without which no society is possible.
It is only along with, and among other human beings
that the individual man attains perfection; — so that
Ethics must be Social Ethics. Friendship therefore is not,
as Aristotle would have it, an expansion of Self-love, but
a limitation of it, or a kind of love of one's neighbour.
And this, like virtue in general, can find a field of exercise only in society, or in citizenship, and not in the

pious monk's renunciation of the world. The hermit, who thinks he is living temperately and righteously, is deceived as to the character of his actions: they may be religious, but moral they certainly are not; and therefore the consideration of them does not belong to Ethics.

Besides, in Ibn Maskawaih's opinion, the Religious Law when rightly apprehended, pre-eminently accords with an Ethics of Benevolence. Religion is a moral training for the people. Its prescriptions, with regard to the worship of God in common and the pilgrimage to Mecca for instance, have plainly in view the cultivation of the love of one's neighbour in the widest acceptation.

In certain special points Ibn Maskawaih has not been successful in combining harmoniously the ethical doctrines of the Greeks, — which he incorporates in his Scheme, — either with one another or with the Law of Islam. That however we pass over; and in any case we ought not only to praise in general terms his attempt to give a system of Ethics which should be free from the casuistry of the Moralists and the asceticism of the Sufis, but also to recognize in the execution of his design the good sense of a man of wide culture.

4. Ibn Sina.

1. Abu Ali al-Hosain ibn Abdallah ibn Sina (*Avicenna*) was born at Efshcno in the neighbourhood of Bokhara, in the year 980, of a family connected with the public service. He received his secular and religious education at home, where Persian and anti-Muslim traditions were still full of life and vigour. Then the youth, precocious alike

in body and in mind, studied philosophy and medicine in Bokhara. He was seventeen years old when he had the good fortune to cure the prince, Nukh ibn Mansur, and to obtain the privilege of access to his library. From that time forward he was his own teacher, in scientific research and in practice, and proved able to turn to account the life and culture of his time. He kept continually venturing his fortunes in the political working of the smaller States: Probably he could never have submitted to a great prince, any more than to a teacher in Science. He wandered on from court to court, at one time employed in State-Administration, at another as a teacher and author, until he became vizir of Shems Addaula in Hamadan. After the death of this prince he was consigned to prison by his son, for some months. He then proceeded farther afield, to the court of Ala Addaula in Ispahan. And at last, having returned to Hamadan, which Ala Addaula had conquered, he died there in 1037, at the age of 57; and there his grave is pointed out to this day.

2. The notion that Ibn Sina pushed on beyond Farabi and reached a purer Aristotelianism, is perhaps the greatest error which has found a footing in the history of Muslim Philosophy. What did this our man of the world in reality care for Aristotle? It was not his concern to commit himself wholly to the spirit of any system. He took what was to his liking, wherever he found it, but he had a preference for the shallow paraphrases of Themistius. Thus he became the great philosopher of accomodation in the East, and the true forerunner of compendium-writers for the whole world. He knew how to group with skill his material, collected as it was from every quarter,

and to present it in an intelligible form, although not
without sophistry. Every moment of his life was fully
employed. In the daytime he attended to State affairs or
gave instruction to his pupils: the evening was devoted
to the social enjoyments of friendship and love; and many
a night found him engaged in composition, pen in hand,
and goblet within reach lest he should fall asleep. Time
and circumstances determined the direction of this activity.
If at the prince's court he had the requisite leisure, and
a library at hand, he wrote his Canon of Medicine or the
great Encyclopaedia of Philosophy. While travelling, he
composed epitomes and smaller works. In prison he wrote
poems and pious meditations, but always in a pleasing
form; in fact his smaller mystical writings have a poetic
charm about them. When commissioned to do so, he put
even Science, Logic and Medicine into verse, — a practice
which came more and more into vogue from the tenth
century onwards. Add to this that he wrote Persian and
Arabic at will, and you get the picture of a most accomplished man. His life was superabundantly rich both in
work and in enjoyment. In geniality, of course he was
inferior to his older compatriot, the poet Firdausi (940—
1020), and in scientific talent to his contemporary Beruni
(v. *infra* § 9), men still of importance in our eyes. Ibn
Sina, however, was the true expression of his time; and
upon this fact have been founded his great influence and
historic position. He did not, like Farabi, withdraw from
common life to become immersed in the commentators of
Aristotle, but he blended in himself Greek science and
Oriental wisdom. Enough commentaries, he thought, had
already been written on the ancient authors: it was now

time for men to construct a philosophy of their own, —
in other words, to give a modern form to the ancient
doctrines.

3. In Medicine Ibn Sina gives diligent endeavour to
produce a systematic account of that science, but here he
proves by no means an exact logician. He assigns a large
place, at least theoretically, to Experience, and describes
in detail the conditions under which alone, for example,
the efficacy of remedies can be ascertained. But the philosophical principles which are involved in Medicine, must
be taken over in the form of lemmas from Philosophy
itself.

Philosophy proper is divided into Logic, Physics and
Metaphysics. In its entirety it embraces the science of all
Existence as such, and of the principles of all the separate
sciences, whereby, as far as is humanly possible, the Soul which
is devoted to philosophy, attains the highest perfection. Now
Existence is either spiritual, when it is the subject of
Metaphysics, or corporeal, when it is discussed in Physics,
or intellectual, when it forms the theme of Logic. The
subjects of Physics can neither exist, nor be thought of
as existing, without Matter. The Metaphysical, however is
quite devoid of Matter; while the Logical is an abstraction
from the Material. The Logical has a certain likeness to
the Mathematical, in so far as the subjects of Mathematics
may also be abstractions from matter. But yet the Mathematical always remains capable of being represented and
constructed, while on the other hand the Logical, as such,
has its existence only in the intellect, as, for instance,
Identity, Unity and Plurality, Universality and Particularity,
Essentiality and Contingency, and so on. Consequently Logic

is the Science of the Determinate Forms of Thought.

In the more detailed treatment of his subject Ibn Sina conforms entirely to Farabi's Logic. This agreement would perhaps be more apparent to us, if the logical works of his predecessor were extant in a more complete form. He frequently lays stress on the defectiveness of the intellectual constitution in man, which is urgently in need of a logical rule. Just as the physiognomist infers from the external features the character of the nature within, so the logician is called upon to derive from known premises that which is unknown. How easy it is for the errors of appearance and desire to insinuate themselves into a process of that kind! A struggle with Sense is required in order that the life of representation may be elevated to the pure truth of the Reason, through which any knowledge of a necessary kind is gained. The divinely-inspired man, but he alone, can dispense with Logic, precisely as the Bedouin is independent of an Arabic Grammar.

The question of Universals is also treated in a manner similar to that which is adopted by Farabi. Prior to any plurality, every thing has an existence in the Mind of God and of the Angels (the Sphere-Spirits); then as material form it enters upon plurality, to be raised finally in the intellect of man to the universality of the Idea. Now just as Aristotle has distinguished between First Substance (Individual) and Second Substance (cogitable as a Universal), so Ibn Sina similarly makes a distinction between First and Second Notion or Intention (*Ma'ná, intentio*). The First is referred to the things themselves, the Second to the disposition of our own thought.

4. In Metaphysics and Physics Ibn Sina is differentiated

from Farabi chiefly through the fact that, by not deriving
Matter from God, he places the Spiritual at a higher
elevation above all that is Material, and in consequence
heightens the importance of the Soul as an intermediary
between the Spiritual and the Corporeal.

From the conception of the Possible and the Necessary,
the existence of a Necessary Being plainly follows. According to Ibn Sina we should not seek to demonstrate the
existence of a Creator from his works, but rather should
deduce, from the possible character of all that is, and all
that is thinkable in the world, the existence of a First
and Necessary Being, whose essence and existence are one.

Not only is every sublunary thing of a 'possible' nature,
but even the heavens are, in themselves, merely 'possible'.
Their existence becomes 'necessary' through another existence which transcends all 'possibility' and therefore all
plurality and mutability. The 'absolutely Necessary' is an
unbending Unity, from which nothing multiplex can
proceed. This first One is the God of Ibn Sina, of whom
many attributes may of course be predicated, such as
thought &c., but only in the sense of negation or relation,
and in such a way that they do not affect the Unity of
his essence.

Out of the first One accordingly, — One only can proceed,
viz., — the first World-Spirit. It is in this latter Spirit that
Plurality has its origin. In fact by thinking of its own
Cause, it generates a third Spirit, the governor of the
outermost Sphere; when again, it thinks of itself, a Soul
is produced, by means of which the Sphere-Spirit exercises its influence; and, in the third place, inasmuch as
it is in itself a 'possible' existence, there emerges from it

a Body, viz., the outermost Sphere. And so the process goes on: Every Spirit, thus generated, except of course the last of the series, liberates from itself a trinity, — Spirit, Soul and Body; for, since the Spirit cannot move the Body directly, it needs the Soul to bring its effectiveness into operation. Finally comes the Active Spirit (*'aql fa''ál*), closing the series, and generating no farther pure (separate) Spirit, but producing and directing the material of what is earthly, as well as corporeal forms and human souls.

The whole of this process, — which is not to be represented as occurring in time, takes place in a substratum, — that of Matter. Matter is the eternal and pure possibility of all that exists, and at the same time the limitation of the operation of the Spirit. It is the principle of all individuality.

Now this teaching must certainly have presented a dreadful appearance to believing Muslims. Mutazilite dialecticians had doubtless asserted that God can do nothing evil, and nothing irrational; but now Philosophy was maintaining that, God instead of being able to do all that is possible is only in a position to effect that which is in its own nature possible, and that only the first World-Spirit proceeds from him directly.

As for the rest Ibn Sina makes every endeavour to conform to the popular belief. Everything exists, he says, through God's appointment, both the Good and the Evil, but it is only the former that meets with his glad approval. Evil is either a non-existent thing, or, — in so far as it proceeds from God, — an accidental thing. Suppose that He, to avoid the evils which of necessity cling to the

world, had kept it from coming into being, — that would
have been the greatest evil of all. The world could not
be better or more beautiful than it actually is. The Divine
Providence, administered as it is by the Souls of the
Heavens, is found in the world's fair order. God and the
pure Spirits know the Universal only, and therefore are
unable to attend to the Particular; but the Souls of the
celestial Spheres, to whose charge falls the representation
of what is individual, and through whom Spirit acts upon
Body, render it possible to admit a providential care for
the individual thing and the individual person, and to
account for revelation, and so on. Farther, the sudden rise
and disappearance of substances (Creation and Annihilation),
in contrast to the constant movement, — that is, the
gradual passing of the Possible into the Actual, — seem
to Ibn Sina to indicate nothing impossible. In general,
there is a predominant want of clearness in his views
regarding the relation of the forms of Existence, — Spirit
and Body, Form and Matter, Substance and Accident. A
place at all events is left for Miracle. In passionate forms
of excitement in the Soul, which often generate in ourselves great heat or cold, we have, according to Ibn Sina,
phenomena analogous to miraculous effects produced by
the World-Soul, although it usually follows the course of
Nature. Our philosopher himself, however, makes a very
moderate use of any of these possibilities. Astrology and
Alchemy he combated on quite rational grounds; and yet
soon after his death astrological poems were attributed to
him; and in Turkish Romance-Literature he appears as a
magician, of course to represent an ancient Mystic.

Ibn Sina's theory of Physics rests entirely on the assumption

that a body can cause nothing. That which *causes*, — is
in every case a Power, a Form, or a Soul, the Spirit
operating through such instrumentality. In the realm of the
Physical there are accordingly countless Powers, the chief
grades of which, from the lower to the higher, are — the
Forces of Nature, the Energies of Plants and Animals,
Human Souls and World-Souls.

5. Farabi was above all things interested in pure Reason:
he loved Thinking for its own sake. Ibn Sina, on the
other hand, is concerned throughout with the Soul. In his
Medicine it is man's Body which he looks to; and similarly, in his Philosophy his eyes are fixed on man's Soul.
The very name of his great Philosophical Encyclopaedia
is — 'The Healing' (that is — of the Soul). His system
centres in Psychology.

His theory of human nature is dualistic. Body and
Soul have no essential connection with one another. All
bodies are produced, under the influence of the stars, from
the mingling of the Elements; and in this way the human
body also is produced, but from a combination in which
the finest proportion is observed. A spontaneous generation
of the body, just like the extinction and restoration of the
human race, is therefore possible. The Soul, however, is
not to be explained from such mixture of the Elements.
It is not the inseparable Form of the body, but is accidental to it. From the Giver of Forms, that is — from
the Active Spirit over us, every Body receives its own
Soul, which is adapted to it and to it alone. From its
very beginning each Soul is an individual substance, and
it developes increasing individuality throughout its life in
the body. It must be admitted that this does not agree

with the contention that Matter is the principle of individuality. But the Soul is the "infant prodigy" of our philosopher. He is not a credulous man, and he often cautions us against too ready an acceptance of mysteries in the life of the Soul; but still he has the art himself of relating many things about the numerous wonderful powers and possible influences of the Soul, as it wanders along the highly intricate pathways of life, and crosses the abysses of Being and Not-Being.

The speculative faculties are the choicest of all the powers of the Soul. Acquaintance with the world is conveyed to the rational soul by the External and Internal Senses. In particular a full account is given by Ibn Sina of his theory of the Internal Senses, or the sensuous-spiritual faculties of representation, which have their seat in the brain.

Medical Philosophers commonly assumed three Internal Senses or stages of the representative process: 1. Gathering the several sense-perceptions into one collective image in the fore part of the brain; 2. Transforming or remodelling this representation of the general Sense, with the help of representations already existing, thus constituting apperception proper, in the middle region; 3. Storing up the 'apperceived' representation in the Memory, which was held to reside in the hinder part of the brain. Ibn Sina, however, carries the analysis somewhat farther. He distinguishes in the anterior portion of the brain the Memory of the Sensible, — or the treasure-house of the collective images, — from the General or Co-ordinating Sense. Farther, he makes out Apperception, — the function of the middle region of the brain, — to be in part brought about uncon-

sciously, under the influence of the sensible and appetent
life, as is the case also with the lower animals, and,
on the other hand, to take place in part consciously, with
the co-operation of the Reason. In the first case the representation preserves its reference to the individual thing, —
thus the sheep knows the hostility of the wolf, — but in
the second case, the representation is extended to the
Universal. Then, in the hinder part of the brain, the Representative Memory, or store-house of the representations
formed by combined Sensuous Impression and Rational
Reflection, follows as a fifth power. In this way five
Internal Senses [1] correspond to the five External Senses,
although with quite another reference than the five Internal
Senses of the Faithful Brethren. The question which is
raised — as to whether one should farther separate Recollection, as a special faculty, from Memory, — remains
unanswered.

6. At the apex of the intellectual powers of the Soul
stands the Reason. There is indeed a Practical Reason also,
but in its action we have been only multiplying ourselves
mediately: On the other hand, in Self-Consciousness, or
the pure recognition of our essential nature, the unity of
our Reason is directly exhibited. But instead of keeping
down the lower powers of the Soul, the Reason lifts them
up, refining Sense-Perception, and generalizing Presentation.
Reason, which at first is a mere capacity for Thought,
becomes elaborated gradually, — in that Material which

[1] [*Translator's note.* — Accordingly Ibn Sina's Five Internal Senses
are: 1. The General or Co-ordinating Sense; 2. Memory of the Collective
sense-images; 3. Unconscious Apperception, referring to individuals; 4.
Conscious Apperception, with generalization; 5. Memory of the higher
apperceptions].

is conveyed to it by the external and internal senses, —
into a finished readiness in Thought. Through exercise the
capability becomes reality. This comes about through the
instrumentality of experience, but under guidance and
enlightenment from above, — from the 'Giver of the Forms',
who as Active Spirit imparts the Ideas to the Reason.
The Soul of man, however, does not possess any memory
for the pure ideas of Reason, for memory always presupposes a corporeal substratum. As often then as the
Rational Soul comes to know anything, that knowledge
flows to it on each occasion from above; and thinking
Souls do not differ in the range and contents of their
knowledge, but in the readiness with which they put
themselves in communication with the Spirit over us, in
order to receive their knowledge.

The Rational Soul, which rules over that which is under
it, and comes to know the higher by means of the enlightenment given by the World-Spirit, is then the real Man,
— brought into existence, but as unmixed essence, as
individual substance, indestructible, immortal. On this
point the clearness of Ibn Sina's teaching marks it off
from that of Farabi; and, since his time, the assumption of
the individual immortality of the human Souls, which have
come into being, is regarded in the East as Aristotelian,
and the opposite doctrine as Platonic. Thus a better understanding prevails between his philosophy and the accepted
religion. The human body and the whole world of sense
furnish the Soul with a school for its training. But after
the death of the body, which puts an end to this body
for ever, the Soul continues to exist in a more or less close
connection with the World-Spirit. In this union with the

Spirit over us, — which is not to be conceived as a complete unification, — the blessedness of the good, 'knowing' souls consists. The lot of the others is eternal misery; for just as bodily defects lead to disease, so punishment is the necessary consequence of an evil condition of Soul. In the same way too, the rewards of Heaven are apportioned according to the degree of soundness or rationality which the Soul has attained in its life on earth .The pure Soul is comforted amidst the sufferings of Time by its prospect of Eternity.

The highest is of course, reached only by a few; for on the pinnacle of Truth there is no room for the many; but one presses forward after another, to reach the source of the knowledge of God, welling forth on its lonely height.

7. To express his view of the Human Reason, Ibn Sina employs and explains poetical traditions, — a favourite proceeding in the Persian literature. First and foremost our interest is awakened by the allegorical figure of Hai ibn Yaqzan. It represents the ascent of the Spirit out of the Elements, and through the realms of Nature, of the Souls, and of the Spirits, up to the throne of the Eternal One. Hai presents himself to the philosopher in the form of an old man with an air of youth about him, and offers his services as guide. The wanderer has been striving to reach a knowledge of Earth and Heaven, by means of his outer and inner senses. Two ways open out before him, one to the West, the way of the Material and the Evil, the other to the Rising Sun, the way of Spiritual and ever-pure Forms; and along that way Hai now conducts him. Together they reach the well of Divine wisdom, the fountain of everlasting youth, where beauty is the curtain of beauty, and light the veil of light, — the Eternal Mystery.

Hai ibn Yaqzan is thus the guide of individual, thinking Souls: he is the Eternal Spirit who is over mankind, and operates in them.

A similar meaning is found by our philosopher in the frequently remodelled late-Greek legend of the brothers Salaman and Absal. Salaman is the World-Man, whose wife (*i. e.*, the World of the Senses) falls in love with Absal, and contrives by a stratagem to wile him into her arms. But before the decisive moment, a flash of lightning comes down from heaven, and reveals to Absal the wantonness of the action which he had nearly committed, and raises him from the world of sensual enjoyment to that of pure spiritual contemplation.

In another passage the soul of the philosopher is compared to a bird, which with great trouble escapes from the snares of the earth, traversing space in its flight, until the Angel of Death delivers it from the last of its fetters.

That is Ibn Sina's Mysticism. His soul has needs, for which his medicine-chest provides no resource, and which the life of a court cannot satisfy.

8 The theoretical development of Ethics and Politics may be left to the teachers of the '*fiqh*'. Our philosopher feels himself on the level of a inspired person, exalted like a God above all human laws. Religious or Civil Law is binding only on the Many. Mohammed's object was, to civilize the Bedouins; and, in order to aid in accomplishing that object, he preached, among other doctrines, that of the Resurrection of the Body. They would never have understood the meaning of purely spiritual blessedness; and so he had to educate them by setting before them the prospect of bodily pleasure or pain. As for the Ascetics, — not-

withstanding their willingness to renounce entirely the
world and the senses, — they chime in with this sensuous
multitude (whose worship of God consists in the obser-
vance of outward forms), in respect that they practise their
works of piety with an eye to a reward also, even though
it be a heavenly one. Higher than the many or the pious
stand those who truly worship God in spiritual love, entertaining neither hope nor fear. Their peculiar possession
is Freedom of the Spirit.

But this secret should not be revealed to the multitude;
and the philosopher confides it only to his favourite pupils.

9. In the course of his travels Ibn Sina met with many
of the learned men of his time; but it would appear that
these interviews did not give rise to any enduring inti-
macies. Just as he feels indebted to Farabi alone, of all
those who preceded him, so the only persons of his own
day, whom he sees fit to thank, are the princes who patronized him. He criticized unfavourably Ibn Maskawaih
(v. IV, 3), whom he met with still more frequently. With
Beruni, his superior in research, he conducted a correspondence, but it was soon broken off.

Beruni (973—1048) deserves a short notice here, to
illustrate the character of the time, although Kindi and
Masudi have a better claim to be called his masters, than
Farabi and the younger Ibn Sina. He was particularly
occupied in the study of Mathematics, Astronomy, Geography and Ethnology; and he was a keen observer and
a good critic. For many a solution of his difficulties, however, he was indebted to Philosophy; and he continually
bestowed attention upon it, as one of the phenomena of
civilization.

Beruni brings into striking prominence the harmony which exists between the Pythagorean-Platonic philosophy, Indian wisdom, and many of the Sufi views. No less striking is his recognition of the superiority of Greek Science, when compared with the attempts and performances of the Arabs and the Indians. 'India', he says, 'not to mention Arabia, has produced no Socrates: there no logical method has expelled phantasy from science'. But yet he is ready to do justice to individual Indians, and he quotes with approval the following, as the teaching of the adherents of Aryabhata: "It is enough for us to know that which is lighted up by the sun's rays. Whatever lies beyond, though it should be of immeasurable extent, we cannot make use of; for what the sunbeam does not reach, the senses do not perceive, and what the senses do not perceive, we cannot know".

From this we may gather what Beruni's philosophy was: Only sense-perceptions, knit together by a logical intelligence, yield sure knowledge; And for the uses of life we need a practical philosophy, which enables us to distinguish friend from foe. He doubtless did not himself imagine that he had said all that could be said on the subject.

10. From the school of Ibn Sina, we have had more names handed down, than we have had writings preserved. Djuzdjani annexes to his Autobiography an account of the life of the master. And, farther, we have one or two short metaphysical treatises by Abu-l-Hasan Behmenyar ibn al-Marzuban, which are nearly in complete agreement with the system of his teacher. But Matter appears to lose somewhat of its substantiality: as Possibility of Existence it becomes a relation of thought.

According to Behmén.yar, God is the pure, uncaused Unity of Necessary Existence, — not the living, all-producing Creator. True enough, He is the cause of the world, but the effect is given necessarily and synchronously with the cause; otherwise the cause would not be perfect, being capable of change. Essentially, though not in point of time, the existence of God precedes that of the world. Three predicates thus pertain to the highest existence, viz, that it is (1) essentially first, (2) self-sufficing, and (3) necessary. In other words God's essential nature is the Necessity of his Existence. All that can possibly be, — owes its existence to this Absolutely Necessary Being.

Now that is quite in harmony with the doctrines of Ibn Sina; and the same is the case with the disciple's scheme of the world and his doctrine of Souls. Whatever has once attained to full reality, — the various Sphere-Spirits according to their kind, Primeval Matter, and the individually different Souls of Men, — all lasts for ever. Nothing that is completely real can pass away, inasmuch as the completely real has nothing to do with mere possibility.

The characteristic of all that is spiritual is its knowledge of its own essential nature. Will is nothing else, in Behmenyar's opinion, than the knowledge of that which is the necessary outcome of that nature. Farther, the life and the joy of rational souls consist in self-knowledge.

11. Ibn Sina achieved a far-reaching influence. His Canon of Medicine was highly esteemed even in the West, from the 13th century to the 16th, and it is still the authority for medical treatment among the Persians of the present day. On Christian Scholasticism his influence was impor-

tant. Dante placed him between Hippocrates and Galen; and Scaliger maintained that he was Galen's equal in Medicine, and much his superior in Philosophy.

For the East he stood and yet stands as the Prince of Philosophy. In that region Neo-Platonic Aristotelianism continues to be known under the form which was given it by Ibn Sina. Manuscripts of his works abound, — an evidence of his popularity, — while commentaries on his writings, and epitomes of them, are countless. He was studied by physicians and statesmen, and even by theologians: It was only a few who went farther back and consulted his sources.

From the very first, of course, he had many enemies, and they were more noisy in their demonstrations than his friends. Poets cursed him: theologians either chimed in with him, or tried to refute him. And in Bagdad in the year 1150, the Caliph Mustandjid consigned to the flames Ibn Sina's writings, as part of a certain judge's philosophical library.

5. Ibn al-Haitham.

1. After the days of Ibn Sina and his school, little more attention was paid to the cultivation of Speculative Philosophy in the Eastern regions of the Muslim empire. In these lands Arabic was forced more and more to yield to Persian, both in life and in literature. That the Persian tongue is not so well adapted for abstract logical and metaphysical discussion — might be only of quite secondary importance, in connection with this decline in speculation; but the conditions of civilization, and with them the subjects which interested men, were sadly changed.

Ethics and Politics came more to the front, although without assuming an actually new form. But in the later Persian literature the predominant place was unmistakeably held by Poetry, partly of a free-thinking tendency, partly, and indeed preponderatingly, of a mystic kind, which satisfied the need for wisdom, experienced by people of culture.

From about the middle of the 10th century, the scientific movement which originated at Bagdad had in part turned westward. We have already found Farabi in Syria, and Masudi in Egypt: In the latter country Cairo was becoming a second Bagdad.

2. In Cairo, at the beginning of the 11th century, we come upon one of the most considerable mathematicians and physicists in all the Middle Ages, Abu Ali Mohammed ibn al-Hasan ibn al-Haitham (*Alhazen*). He had formerly been a government-official in Basra, his native town. Confiding too much in the practical value of his mathematical knowledge, he imagined that he could regulate the inundations of the Nile; but having been summoned on that account by the Caliph al-Hakim, he became aware, soon after his arrival, of the futility of his efforts. Thereupon he fell into disgrace as a public official, and went into hiding till the Caliph's death, in 1021. From that time he devoted himself to literary and scientific work, up to his own death, in 1038.

His chief strength is shown in mathematics and its practical application; but he also devoted great attention to the writings of Galen and Aristotle, nor did he confine that attention to the physical treatises. By his own confession he had, in a spirit of doubt about everything, been engaged, from his youth up, in considering the various views and doctrines of men, until he came to recognize in all of them more or less successful attempts to approximate to the truth. Moreover truth for him was only that which was presented as material for the faculties of sense-perception, and which received its form from the understanding, being thus the logically-elaborated perception. To seek such truth was his aim in the study of philosophy. In his view philosophy should be the basis of all the sciences. He found it in the writings of Aristotle, inasmuch as that sage had best understood how to knit sense-perception into a coherent whole with rational knowledge. With eagerness therefore he studied and illustrated Aristotle's works, for the use and profit of mankind, as well as to exercise his own intellect and provide a treasure and consolation for his old age. Of these labours, however, nothing seems to have been preserved for us.

The most important of Ibn al-Haitham's writings is the "Optics", which has come down to us in a Latin translation and redaction. In it he shows himself to be an acute mathematical thinker, always taking pains with the analysis of hypotheses and of the actual examples. A Western, belonging to the 13th century (Vitello), was able to give a more methodical account of the whole subject; but yet in keenness of observation on specific points, Ibn al-Haitham may be reckoned his superior.

3. Ibn al-Haitham's thinking is expressed in quite a mathematical style. The Substance of a body consists, according to him, of the sum of its essential attributes, just as a whole is equal to the sum of its parts, and a concept to the sum of its marks.

In the "Optics" the psychological remarks on Seeing and on Sense-Perception in general — are of special interest for us. Here he exerts himself to separate the individual Moments of the Perception, and to give prominence to the condition of Time as characterizing the whole process.

Perception then is a compound process, arising out of (1) sensation, (2) comparison of several sensations or of the present sensation with the memory-image which has been gradually formed in the soul as a result of earlier sensations, and (3) recognition, in such fashion that we recognize the present percept as equivalent to the memory-image. Comparison and recognition are not activities of the Senses, which merely receive impressions passively, but they devolve upon the Understanding as the faculty of judgment. Ordinarily the whole process goes forward unconsciously or semi-consciously, and it is only through reflection that it is brought within our consciousness, and that the apparently simplex is separated into its component parts.

The process of Perception is gone through very quickly. The more practice a man has in this respect, and the oftener a perception is repeated, the more firmly is the memory-image stamped upon the soul, and the more rapidly is recognition or perception effected. The cause of this is that the new sensation is supplemented by the image which is already present in the soul. One might thus be disposed to think that Perception was an instantaneous act, at least after long practice. That, however, would be erroneous, for not only is every sensation attended by a corresponding change localized in the sense-organ, which demands a certain time, but also, between the stimulation of the organ and the consciousness of the perception an interval of time must elapse, corresponding to the transmission of the stimulus for some distance along the nerves. That it needs time, for example, to perceive a colour, is proved by the rotating circle of colours, which shows us merely a mixed colour, because on account of the rapid movement we have no time to perceive the individual colours.

Comparison and Recognition are, according to Ibn al-Haitham, the significant Mental Moments of Perception. On the other hand Sensation 'tallies with the Material; and the Sense experiencing the sensation exhibits a passive attitude. Properly all sensation is in itself a kind of discomfort, which ordinarily does not make itself felt, but which emerges into consciousness under very strong stimuli, for example, through too bright a light. A pleasurable character accrues only to the completed perception, that is to the recognition which lifts the material given in sensation, up to the mental form.

The comparison and recognition, which are put in operation in Perception, constitute an unconscious judgment and conclusion. The child is already drawing a conclusion, when of two apples he chooses the finer one. As often as we comprehend a connection, we are concluding. But, since judging and concluding are quickly settled, men are easily misled in this matter, and frequently they regard as an original concept that which is merely a judgment derived by a process of ratiocination. In the case of everything which is announced to us as an axiom, we should be on our guard and trace it up, to see whether it cannot be derived from something more simple.

4. This appeal of our philosopher had little effect in the

East. It is true that in Mathematics and Astronomy he created somewhat of a school; but his Aristotelian philosophy had comparatively few admirers. We know only one of his scholars who is counted among the Philosophers, Abu-l-Wafa Mubasshir ibn Fatik al-Qaid, an Egyptian emir, who in the year 1053 produced a work made up of proverbial wisdom, anecdotes in illustration of the history of philosophy, and so on. Hardly anything can be traced in it which is the result of his own thinking. It should have been pleasant reading. And the inhabitants of Cairo in after times found edification, — more even than in such a work, — in the tales of the Thousand and One Nights.

The East set the stigma of heresy upon Ibn al-Haitham and his works, and now it has almost completely forgotten him. A disciple of Maimonides, the Jewish philosopher, relates that he was in Bagdad on business, when the library of a certain philosopher, (who died in 1214) was burned there. The preacher, who conducted the execution of the sentence, threw into the flames, with his own hands, an astronomical work of Ibn al-Haitham, after he had pointed to a delineation therein given of the sphere of the earth, as an unhappy symbol of impious Atheism.

V. THE OUTCOME OF PHILOSOPHY IN THE EAST.

1. GAZALI.

1. We have already seen that the theological movement in Islam was strongly influenced by Philosophy. Not only the Mutazilite, but also the Antimutazilite Dialectic drew its opinions and the arguments with which it supported its own teaching or disputed that of its opponents, for the most part out of the writings of the philosophers. Out of these one took just what he was able to make use of: the rest he left in peace, or else he endeavoured to refute it. Thus numerous writings came into existence, directed against some particular philosophical doctrine, or some individual philosopher. No attempt, however, had been made before the time of Gazali, to direct an attack from general points of view and after thorough-going study, against the entire system of Philosophy which had been built up in the East on a Greek foundation.

Gazali's undertaking had also a positive side. Along with the Dialectic which sought to make the doctrines of the Faith intelligible, or even to provide them with a rational basis, there were movements in Islam of a mysticism which tended to a conception of dogma, profound and full of feeling. Its wish was, not to comprehend or

demonstrate the contents of the Faith, but to learn them
by experience and live in them through the Spirit. The
highest certitude ought to belong to the Faith. Ought it
then to be in the power of any to transform it into a
derived knowledge? Or must its tenets be principles of the
Reason, neither capable of farther proof, nor requiring it?
But the fundamental principles of the Reason, when once
they are known, must be universally recognized; and universal recognition is lacking in the case of the tenets of
the Faith. From what other source does unbelief arise?
Thus the questioning proceeded; and it seemed to many
that the only way out of these doubts was to base religious doctrine upon an inner, supra-rational illumination.
At first this came about unconsciously, under a mystic
impulse, whereby the contents of moral and religious
teaching were often brought into neglect. Gazali took part
in this movement also. That which had perhaps been
typified by the Salimites and Karramites, Antimutazilite
sects, he set forth completely and in a dignified style;
and ever since his time Mysticism both sustains and crowns
the Temple of Learning in Orthodox Islam.

2. The story of this man's life is a remarkable one;
and, in order to understand the effectiveness of his work,
it is absolutely essential to examine it with a measure of
detail. He was born at Tos in Khorasan in the year 1059,
being thus a countryman of the great poet Firdausi. And
just as the latter furnishes a proof of the old glory of the
Persian nation, so Gazali was destined to be a "testimony
and ornament" for all future Islam. Even his early education, — obtained after his father's death, in the house
of a Sufi friend, — was rather cosmopolitan than national

in its direction. Farther, any limitation was displeasing to the youth's restless and fanciful spirit. He did not feel at home in the hair-splitting casuistry of the teachers of Morals with their precise formulas: he regarded it as a worldly knowledge, from which he turned away, to immerse his spirit in the knowledge of Allah. Then he studied theology in Nishabur with the Imām al-Haramain, who died in 1085; and at the same time he may himself have begun to write and to teach, and, perhaps even thus early, to entertain doubts of his own science. Thereafter he was in attendance at the court of Nizam al-Mulk, the Vizir of the Seldjuk prince, until in 1091 he was appointed a Professor in Bagdad. It was during this time at all events that he busied himself most with philosophy. But it was not pure love for the science, which impelled him to that study, but the longing of his heart to find a solution of the doubts which assailed his understanding. Not any explanation of the events of the world, nor any clearing up of his own thinking, but peace of mind and the experience of a higher reality constituted the object which he strove to reach. He subjected to a thorough study the writings of the philosophers, in particular those of Farabi and Ibn Sina; and, following chiefly the system of the latter, he composed a Compendium of Philosophy, regarding it objectively, but still with some appearance of sympathy with its contents. He said, — at first in a kind of whisper to pacify his own mind, but afterwards publicly in self-defence, — that he composed that work in order that he might follow up the statement of the doctrines of philosophy with the refutation of the same. And that refutation did appear, probably not long after. It was the famous

"Destruction of the Philosophers", — which was composed in all likelihood while he was still in Bagdad, or shortly after he had left it.

But by the end of four years, viz in 1095, Gazali had discontinued his work of teaching in Bagdad, attended though it had been with outward success. His mind, continually in a state of doubt, probably found no satisfaction in dogmatic prelections. He was alternately attracted and repelled by his own brilliant position, and he came to think that he could, and that he should, fight against the world and its wisdom in some other way, to more purpose. Ambition with him embraced far more than this world. Profounder still his musings became; and during an illness of his, the inner call presented itself to his soul. He had secretly to prepare for the work, by means of Sufi exercises, perhaps even to assume the character of a religious and political reformer. At the very time that the Crusaders were equipping themselves in the West against Islam, Gazali was preparing himself to be the spiritual champion of the Muslim faith. His conversion was not of a violent character, like that of St. Augustine, but was rather to be compared to the experience of St. Jerome, who was summoned in a dream from his Ciceronian predilections to practical Christianity.

For ten years Gazali travelled here and there, dividing his time between pious exercises and literary work. In the first part of that period it may be conjectured that he wrote his principal theologico-ethical work, "The Revival of Religious Sciences": towards the end he endeavoured to exercise influence as a reformer. His journeyings led him by way of Damascus and Jerusalem — before it was taken

by the Crusaders, — Alexandria, Mecca and Medina, back
to his home.

After his return Gazali once more engaged in teaching
for a short time in Nishabur; and he died in Tos, his native
town, on the 19th of December, 1111. His closing years
were chiefly devoted to pious contemplation and the study
of the Traditions, which as a youth he could never remember.
A beautifully complete and rounded life, in which the end
comes back to the beginning!

3. Gazali passes in review the spiritual tendencies of his
time. These are: the Dialectic of the Theologians; Sufi
Mysticism; Pythagorean Popular Philosophy; and Neo-
Platonic Aristotelianism. That which Dialectic desires to
establish is also the object of his own faith; but its arguments appear to him rather weak, and many of its assertions on that account open to question. He feels most in
sympathy with the Sufi Mysticism: to it he owes his
dearest possession, viz, the establishment of his own faith
in Personality, — so that he can postulate as an inner
experience that which the Dialecticians attempt to derive
by a process of reasoning. He thanks also the Popular
Philosophy for the instruction it gives, particularly in
Mathematics, which he fully recognizes as a science, together with its Astronomical deductions. He concedes the
validity of its Physics, where that is not in conflict with
the Faith. But Aristotelianism, — as it has been taught
by Farabi and Ibn Sina, with as much subservience to
authority as has been exhibited by the Theologians, —
seems to him to be the enemy of Islam; and in the name
of all the Muslim schools and tendencies of thought together, he feels bound to do battle with it, as from a

catholic standpoint. And in truth he does this with Aristotle's own weapons, — those of Logic; for the axioms of thought which Logic lays down are, in his eyes, just as firmly established as the propositions of Mathematics. Fully alive to this, he starts from the Principle of Contradiction, to which, according to his contention, God himself submits. Of the Physico-Metaphysical doctrines of Philosophy then, he attacks three in particular: 1. That the world is eternal; 2. That God takes cognizance only of the Universal, and that consequently there is no special providence; 3. That the Soul alone is immortal, and therefore a Resurrection of the Body is not to be looked for. In the refutation of these doctrines Gazali is in many respects dependent on the Christian commentator on Aristotle, Johannes Philoponus, who also has written against the doctrine of the eternity of the world maintained by Proclus.

4. (1) The world, according to the philosophers, is a sphere of finite extent but of infinite duration. From all eternity, it proceeds from God, even as the effect is in existence at the same time with the cause. Gazali, on the contrary, is of opinion that it is not admissible to put such different constructions on the notions of Space and Time respectively; and he holds that the Divine Causality should be defined as free Creative Might.

First then as to Space and Time: we are as little able to imagine an outermost boundary of Space as a beginning or end of Time. He who believes in an endless Time, must, in consistency with that notion of his, assume also the existence of an infinite Space. To say that Space answers to the external sense, and Time on the other hand to the internal, — does not alter the case, for we

do not after all get rid of the Sensible. Just as Space
bears a relation to Body, so does Time to the movement
of Body. Both are merely relations of things, created in
and with the things of the world, or rather relations
between our conceptions, which God creates in us.

Still more important is that which Gazali advances about
Causality. The Philosophers distinguish between an operation of God, of Spiritual Beings endowed with will, of the
Soul, of Nature, of Chance and the like; but for Gazali,
just as for the orthodox Kalam, there is really only one
causality, that of the 'Willing' Being. He completely puts
aside the causality of Nature, which is reducible without
remainder into a relation of Time. We see one definite
phenomenon (Cause) regularly succeeded by another definite
phenomenon (Effect); but how the latter results from the
former is left an enigma for us. Of operation in the objects
of Nature we know nothing. Farther, any alteration is in
itself inconceivable. That any one thing should become a
different thing is incomprehensible to thought, which may
just as well ask about facts as about causes. A thing
either exists, or it does not exist; but not even Divine
Omnipotence can transform one existing thing into another
thing. It creates or else annihilates.

And yet it is a fact of our consciousness that we do
effect something. If we 'will' anything, and possess the
power to carry it out, we claim the result as our act.
Action, proceeding from a free will, and conscious of the
exertion of power, is the only causality of which we know;
aud we argue from this to the Divine Being. But by what
right? The warrant for such a conclusion Gazali thinks
that he finds in his own personal experience of the image

of God in his soul; while on the other hand he declines
to credit Nature with the likeness to God which belongs
to his own soul.

For him accordingly, God, in so far as he can be
known from the world, is the Almighty Being, free in
will and efficient in operation. No spatial limit may be
set to his causative activity, which yet the philosophers do,
when they grant only his influence in his first created work.
But on the other hand He can limit his own work both
in Space and Time, so that this finite world has only a
finite duration. That God should call the world into existence out of nothing by an absolute act of creation —
seems to the Philosophers to be absurd. They recognize
only an exchange of Accidents or Forms in the one material, a passing of the actual from possibility to possibility. But does nothing new ever come then into being?
Is not every apprehension of the senses, — asks Gazali, —
and every spiritual perception, something entirely new,
which either exists or else does not exist, but at whose
coming into existence the contrary does not cease, and at
whose vanishing from existence, the opposite does not
make its appearance? Consider farther the numerous individual souls which, according to Ibn Sina's system, must
be in existence: have not these come into being, absolutely new?

There is no end to the putting of questions. The representative process wanders about in all directions and far;
and thought leads us on *ad infinitum*. The chain of cau-
sation can nowhere be brought to an end, any more than
Space or Time. In order then that there should be a
definite, final Existence, — and in postulating this, Gazali

is at one with the Philosophers —, we need an Eternal Will as First Cause, different from everything else.

We may at all events make this acknowledgement to Gazali, that Ibn Sina's fantastic doctrine of Forms and Souls makes no stand against his criticism.

5. (2) We have now come to the idea of God. In the view of the Philosophers, God is the highest Being, and his essence is Thought. That which He knows, comes into existence, emanating from his abundance; but he has not positively 'willed' it, for all Willing presupposes a deficiency, — a need —, and is conditioned by some change in the Being that wills. Willing is movement in the material: completely real Spirit wills nothing. Therefore God beholds his creation in a contemplation which is undisturbed by any wish. He recognizes himself, or even his first Creature, or, according to Ibn Sina, the Universal, the eternal Genera and Species of all things.

But according to Gazali there must eternally belong to God a Will, as one of his eternal attributes. In a conventional way he grants, it is true, that in metaphysical and ethical considerations knowing precedes willing, but he is convinced that unity of Being does not more reside in knowing than in willing. Not only the multiplicity of the objects of knowledge, and their different relations to the knowing Subject, but even Self-Consciousness, or knowing about the knowing, considered *per se*, is an endless process. An act of will is absolutely necessary to bring it to a conclusion. In directing the attention and in self-communing an original "Willing" is in operation; and thus even Divine knowledge comes to a conclusion as a coherent unity, in its Personality, by means of an original eternal Will. In place of the assertion of the Philosophers that God wills the world, because he thinks of it as the best, Gazali substitutes the statement: "God has cognizance of the world because he wills it and in his willing it".

Must not then He, who wills and creates all, have cognizance of his work down to the smallest part of its material? Just as his eternal will is the cause of all individual things, so his eternal knowledge embraces at one and the same time every particular thing, without the unity of his nature being thereby taken away. There is consequently a Providence.

To the objection that Divine Providence makes every particular event a necessary event, Gazali, like St. Augustine, replies that this fore-knowledge is not distinguishable from knowledge in memory, — that is to say, that God's knowledge is exalted above every distinction of time.

It may be questioned whether, in order to save the eternal, almighty, creative Will, Gazali has not sacrificed to that absolute might both the temporary character of the world, which he would like to prove, and the freedom of human action, from which he sets out, and which he would not altogether surrender. This world of shadows and images, as he calls it, vanishes for the sake of God.

6. (3) The third question, with regard to which Gazali separates himself from the Philosophers, has less philosophic interest. It refers to the Resurrection of the Body. According to the Philosophers it is only the Soul that is immortal, either in its individuality or as a part of the World-Soul: The Body on the other hand is perishable. Against this Dualism, which in theory led to an ascetic Ethics, but which in practice was easily converted into

Libertinism, the religious and moral feeling of Gazali rose in rebellion. If the flesh is to have its obligations, it must in turn be invested with its rights. The possibility of the Resurrection cannot be denied, for the reunion of the Soul with its (new) bodily frame is not more wonderful than its first union with the earthly body, which has been assumed even by the Philosophers. Surely then every soul at the resurrection-time may obtain a new body suited to it. But in any case Man's real essence is the Soul; and it is of little consequence what the material is, out of which its heavenly body is formed.

7. Even from these last propositions it is clear that Gazali's theology did not remain unaffected by philosophical speculation. Like the Fathers of the Western Church, he had, whether consciously or unconsciously, appropriated a good deal from philosophy; and for that reason his theology was long proscribed as a heretical innovation by the Muslims of the West. In reality his teaching regarding God, the World, and the human Soul exhibits many elements which are foreign to the oldest type of Islam, and which may be traced back, — partly through the intervening agency of Christian and Jewish writers and partly through that of more recent Muslim authors, — to heathen wisdom.

Allah, Lord of the Worlds, God of Mohammed, is for Gazali a living personality it is true, but yet far less anthropomorphic than he appeared to simple Faith or in the Antimutazilite dogma. The surest way of coming to know him must be to refuse to attribute to him any of the properties of his creatures. But that does not mean that he posssesses no attributes: the very reverse is the case. The plurality of his qualities does not prejudice the Unity

of his Being. Analogies are presented in the bodily world:
A thing certainly cannot be both black and white at the
same time, but it may well be cold and also dry. Only,
if the qualities of men are attributed to God, they must
be understood in another and higher sense, for he is pure
Spirit. Besides omniscience and omnipotence, pure goodness
and omnipresence belong to Him. By means of this omnipresence this world and the next are brought in a manner
nearer to one another than by the usual representation.

The conception of God is thus spiritualized. But resurrection and the future life are also regarded as being much
more spiritual in character than the present life. Such a
conception is facilitated by the doctrine of the Gnostic
Philosophy, that there are three or four worlds. One above
the other in regular order rise the Earthly and Sensible
World of Men, the World of Celestial Spirits, to which
our Soul belongs, the World of Supra-celestial Angels, and
lastly God himself, as the World of purest Light and most
perfect Spirit. The pious and enlightened Soul ascends
from the lower world through the heavens till it is face
to face with God, for it is of spiritual nature and its
resurrection-body is of celestial essence.

In a manner corresponding to the different worlds and
grades of Souls, men themselves differ from one another.
The man of sensuous nature must be content with the
Koran and Tradition: he should not venture beyond the
letter of the Law. The study of duty is his bread of life;
philosophy would be a deadly poison to him. He who
cannot swim should not venture into the sea.

However there are always people who go into the water
for the purpose of learning to swim. They want to elevate

their faith into knowledge, but in the process they may easily fall into doubt and unbelief. For them, in Gazali's opinion, a usefal remedy may be found in the study of Doctrine and Polemics directed against Philosophy.

Those, however, have reached the highest degree of human perfection, who, without any laborious cogitation, experience in themselves by means of an inward and Divine illumination the truth and the reality of the Spiritual World. Such are the prophets and pious mystics, among whom Gazali himself may be reckoned. They see God in everything, — Him, and Him alone —, and in Nature just as in the life of their own Soul; but they see Him best in the Soul, for although it is not Divine it has at least a likeness to the Divine. How altered now is every outward thing! That which seems to be in existence outside of us, becomes a condition or a property of the Soul, which in the consciousness of its union with God, advances to the highest bliss. All things then become one in Love. The true service of God transcends fear of punishment and hope of reward, attaining to Love of God in the Spirit. The perfect servant of God is raised above endurance and thanksgiving, — which constitute the obligation of the pious wanderer upon the earth, so long as he remains imperfect —, so that even in this world he loves and praises God with joy of heart.

8. From what has been said it follows that there are three stages of Belief or Certainty: *First*, the belief of the multitude, who believe what some man worthy of belief declares to them, for instance, that So-and-so is in the house; *secondly*, the knowledge of the learned, gained by deduction: they have heard So-and-so speaking,

and conclude that he is in the house; but *thirdly* we have
the immediate certainty of the 'knowing' ones, for they
have entered the house and seen the person with their
own eyes.

In contradistinction to the Dialecticians and Philosophers,
Gazali everywhere lays stress upon experience. The former,
with their Universal Ideas, in the first place fail to do
justice to the multiplicity which attaches to this world of
sense. The sensible qualities of things, — even the number
of the stars for example, — we come to know only through
experience, and not from pure Ideas. Much less, however,
do such Ideas exhaust the heights and depths of our inner
being. That which the friend of God knows intuitively,
remains hidden for ever from the discursive intellect of
the learned. A very small number attain to this height
of knowledge, where they meet with the Apostles of God
and Prophets of all times. It is the duty then of the
Spirits who stand at a lower level to strive to follow them.

But now how are we to recognize the superior Spirit
whom we need as our guide? That is a question, on which
every religiously-determined system, which cannot do without human intermediaries, must founder, if considered
purely in the light of the understanding. Even Gazali's
answer is indecisive This much is certain to him, that
grounds furnished by the reason alone cannot decide this
question. The Prophet and Teacher who has been actually
inspired by God is recognized by merging ourselves in his
peculiar personality, through the experience of an inward
relationship. The truth of Prophecy is authenticated by the
moral influence which it exercises upon the Soul. Of the
truthfulness of God's word in the Koran we acquire a

moral, not a theoretical certainty. The detached miracle is not capable of convincing; but the revelation as a whole, together with the personality of the Prophet, through whom the revelation has been conveyed, produce an irresistible impression upon the kindred soul. Then, wholly carried away by such impression, the soul renounces the world, to walk in the way of God.

9. Gazali is without doubt the most remarkable figure in all Islam. His doctrine is the expression of his own personality. He abandoned the attempt to understand this world. But the religious problem he comprehended much more profoundly than did the philosophers of his time. These were intellectual in their methods, like their Greek predecessors, and consequently regarded the doctrines of Religion as merely the products of the conception or fancy or even caprice of the lawgiver. According to them Religion was either blind obedience, or a kind of knowledge which contained truth of an inferior order.

On the other hand Gazali represents Religion as the experience of his inner Being. It is for him more than Law and more than Doctrine: it is the Soul's experience.

It is not every one who has this experience of Gazali's. But even those who cannot follow him in his mystic flight, when he transcends the conditions of any possible experience, will at least be constrained to acknowledge that his aberrations in searching for the highest are not less important for the history of the Human Mind than the apparently surer paths taken by the philosophers of his time, through a land which others had discovered before them.

2. The Epitomists.

1. In a history of scholarly Education as conducted in the Muslim nations, this subject would necessarily have a larger space assigned it : but here we shall dismiss it in a few words.

That Gazali has annihilated philosophy in the East, for all time to come, is an assertion frequently repeated but wholly erroneous, and one which evidences neither historical knowledge nor understanding. Philosophy in the East has since his day numbered its teachers and students by hundreds and by thousands. The teachers of the Faith have no more discontinued their dialectical arguments in support of Doctrine than the teachers of Morals have abandoned their hair-splitting casuistry. General culture too has adopted an element of philosophical learning.

But it is true that Philosophy did not succeed in conquering for itself a commanding position, or in retaining the consideration which it once enjoyed. According to an Arab anecdote a Philosopher, who had been thrown into prison, on being asked what he was fit for, by a man who wanted to purchase him as a slave, is said to have replied: "For freedom". Philosophy needs freedom. And where was this Freedom to be met with in the East? Freedom from material cares, freedom to exemplify unprejudiced thinking, tended continually to dwindle away from regions where no enlightened despots were to be found, able to warrant and protect it. But that is just a symptom of the general decay of civilization. And although travellers from the West in the twelfth century praised highly the culture of the East, it had, in comparison with earlier times, at least begun to decline. In no department

did they pass the mark which had been reached of old:
Minds were now too weak to accomplish such a feat.
Literary production became stagnant, and the only merit
which belongs to the voluminous compilers of the following
centuries is that of elegant selection. Ethical and religious
doctrine had ended in Mysticism; and the same was the case
with Philosophy. After the time of Ibn Sina, the Prince of
Philosophy, no one felt called upon to come forward with
independent views. The day had come for Abridgements,
Commentaries, Glosses, and Glosses upon Glosses. The
learned world occupied their time in school with work of
that nature, while the believing multitude placed themselves
more and more under the guidance of the Dervish orders.

2. That which general education borrowed most from
philosophical Propaedeutics was a little Mathematics &c.,
naturally exceedingly elementary as a rule. By sectaries
and mystics a good deal was taken over from Pythagorean-
Platonic wisdom. In particular these doctrines had to be
drawn upon in order to support the belief in saints and
miracles; and a barren syncretistic Theosophy was tricked
out therewith. The system even enrolled Aristotle among
its teachers, of course the spurious Aristotle, but it turned
him into a disciple of Agathodaemon and Hermes.

The more sober-minded thinkers, on the other hand,
kept to Aristotelianism, so far as it agreed with their own
views or with the orthodox Faith. The system of Ibn Sina
was almost universally followed by them; and it was only
a few that went back to Farabi, or that endeavoured to
combine the two. Very little notice was taken of Physical
and Metaphysical doctrines: Ethics and Politics were rather
more attended to. Logic was the only subject universally

studied; for it could be admirably conveyed in scholastic form; and, as pure Formal Logic, it was an instrument which every one was able to make use of. In fact with the resources of Logic everything might be proved; and even if the demonstration should be recognized as faulty, there was this consolation that the averment might still be true, although its demonstration had not been properly conducted.

Even in the Encyclopaedia of Abu Abdallah al-Khwarizmi, a production of the last quarter of the tenth century, a larger space was assigned to Logic than to Physics and Metaphysics. The very same thing was done in many later encyclopaedias and compilations. The Dogmatists also commenced their system with logical and epistemological considerations, in which a traditional eulogy was pronounced over "knowing". And from the twelfth century onwards there arose a whole multitude of separate arrangements of the Aristotelian Organon. Here may be mentioned only, — as being much used, commented on, and so forth, — the works of Abhari († 1264), who gave a short summary of the whole 'Logic' under the title of "Isagudji" (εἰσαγωγή); and the works of Qazwini († 1276).

At the greatest University in the Muslim world, that of Cairo, the Epitomes of the 13th and 14th centuries are used, up to this day. There the word still is, as for a long time it was with ourselves: "First of all a College of Logic", and, we need scarcely add, with no better result. They indulge themselves, within the limits of the Law, in the luxury of studying the rules of thinking discovered by the ancient philosophers, but all the while they smile at these men and at the Mutazilite Dialecticians, who "believed in Reason!"

VI. PHILOSOPHY IN THE WEST.

1. BEGINNINGS.

1. Western North-Africa, Spain and Sicily are reckoned as forming the Muslim West. North-Africa, to begin with, is of subordinate importance: Sicily is regulated by Spain, and is soon overthrown by the Normans of Lower Italy. For our purpose Muslim Spain or Andalusia first falls to be considered.

The drama of culture in the East passes here through a second representation. Just as Arabs there intermarried with Persians, so in the West they intermarry with Spaniards. And instead of Turks and Mongols we have here the Berbers of North-Africa, whose rude force is flung into the play of more refined civilization with a blighting influence ever on the increase.

After the fall of the Omayyads in Syria (750), a member of that House, Abderrakhman ibn Moawiya, betook himself to Spain, where he contrived to work his way up to the dignity of Emir of Cordova and all Andalusia. This Omayyad overlordship lasted for more than 250 years, and after a passing system of petty States, it attained its greatest brilliancy under Abderrakhman III (912—961), the first who assumed the title of Caliph, and his son al-Hakam II (961—976). The tenth century was for Spain, what the ninth was for the East, — the time of highest material and intellectual civilization. If possible, it was more fresh and native here than in the East, and, if it be true that all theorizing betokens either a lack or a stagnation of the power of production, it was more productive also: The sciences, and Philosophy in particular, had far fewer representatives in Spain. Speaking generally, we may say that the relations of intellectual life took a simpler form. There was a smaller number of strata in the new culture than in the old. No doubt there were, besides Muslims, Jews and Christians in Spain, who in the time of Abderrakhman III played their part in this cultivated life, of the Arabic stamp, in common with the rest. But of adherents of Zoroaster, atheists and such like, there were none. Even the sects of Eastern Islam were almost unknown. Only one school of Law, that of Malik, was admitted. No Mutazilite dialectic troubled the peace of the Faith. True enough the Andalusian poets glorified the trinity of Wine, Woman and Song; but flippant free-thinking on the one hand, and gloomy theosophy and renunciation of the world on the other, rarely found expression.

On the whole, intellectual culture was dependent upon the East. From the tenth century onwards many journeys in search of knowledge were undertaken thither from Spain, by way of Egypt and as far as Eastern Persia, for the purpose of attending the prelections of scholars of renown. And farther, educational requirements in Andalusia attracted to it many a learned Eastern who found no occupation in his own home. Besides, al-Hakam II caused books to be copied, all over the East, for his library, which is said to have contained 400,000 volumes.

The West was mainly interested in Mathematics, Natural Science, Astrology and Medicine, precisely as was the case at first in the East. Poetry, History and Geography were cultivated with ardour. But the mind was not yet "sicklied o'er with the pale cast of thought", for when Abdallah ibn Masarra of Cordova, under Abderrakhman III, brought home with him from the East a system of Natural Philosophy, he had to submit to see his writings consigned to the flames.

2. In the year 1013 Cordova, "the Gem of the World", was laid waste by the Berbers, and the kingdom of the Omayyads was split up into a number of minor States. Its second bloom fills up the eleventh century, — the Medicean age of Spain, in which Art and Poetry still flourish in luxuriant growth at the courts of the various cities, upon the ruins of ancient splendour. Art grows refined; poetry becomes sage, and scientific thought subtle. Intellectual nutriment continues to be fetched from the East; and Natural Philosophy, the writings of the Faithful Brethren, and Logic from the school of Abu Sulaiman al-Sidjistani find admission one after the other. Towards the close of the century it is possible to trace the influence even of the writings of Farabi, and the "Medicine" of Ibn Sina becomes known.

The beginnings of philosophical reflection are found chiefly with the numerous men of culture among the Jews. Eastern Natural Philosophy produces a powerful and quite singular impression upon the mind of Ibn Gebirol, the Avencebrol of Christian authors; and Bakhya ibn Pakuda is influenced by the Faithful Brethren. Even the religious poetry of the Jews is affected by the philosophical movement; and what speaks therein is not the Jewish Congregation seeking after God, but the Soul rising towards the Supreme Spirit.

Among the Muslims, however, the number of those who addressed themselves to a thorough study of Philosophy was very limited. No master gathered about him a numerous band of disciples; and meetings of the learned, for the discussion of philosophical subjects, were scarcely ever held. The individual thinker must have felt very lonely in these circumstances. In the West, just as in the East, Philosophy was developed subjectively; but here it was more the concern of a few isolated individuals; and, besides, it stood more apart from the faith of the mass of the people. In the East there were countless intermediary agencies between faith and knowledge, — between the philosophers and the believing community. The problem of the individual thinker, confronted by political society and the faith of narrow-minded fanatical multitudes, was accordingly realized more acutely in the West.

2. IBN BADDJA.

1. Towards the end of the eleventh century, when Abu Bekr Mohammed ibn Yakhya ibn al-Saig ibn Baddja (*Avempace*) was born in Saragossa, the fair kingdom of Andalusia was approaching the time of its disappearance in a system of petty States. It was threatened from the North by the less civilized but yet powerful and brave Christian knights. But the Berber dynasty of the Almoravids came to the

rescue, who were not only firmer in the faith but also wiser in their policy than the voluptuous ruling race of Spain. Then the time of refined culture and free enquiry seemed gone for ever. Only traditionalists, of the strictest rite, ventured to make a public appearance, while philosophers, unless they kept concealed, were persecuted or put to death.

2. But barbarous lords have their caprices, being fond of appropriating, at least superficially, the culture of those who have been subjugated by them. Thus Abu Bekr ibn Ibrahim, brother-in-law of the Almoravid prince Ali, — who was for some time Governor of Saragossa, made Ibn Baddja his intimate friend and first minister, thereby giving great offence to his *Faqihs* and soldiers. Now this was a man, skilled both in the theory and practice of the Mathematical Sciences, particularly Astronomy and Music, as well as an adept in Medicine, and one who was devoted to speculative studies in Logic, Natural Philosophy and Metaphysics; and in the opinion of the fanatics he was an utterly abandoned atheist and immoral person.

We know nothing more of the outward life of Ibn Baddja except that he was in Seville in the year 1118, after the fall of Saragossa, and that he composed several of his works there, afterwards betaking himself to the Almoravid court in Fez, where he died in 1138. According to tradition he met his death by poison, administered at the instigation of a jealous physician. His short life, as he himself confesses, had not been a happy one; and he had often longed for death, as a final refuge. Material want, and, above all, intellectual isolation, may have weighed down his spirits. His extant writings abundantly evince that he was unable to feel at home in that day and that environment.

3. He conforms almost entirely to Farabi, the quiet, solitary Eastern. Like him he was little given to systematizing. His original treatises are but few in number; and they consist chiefly of brief expositions of Aristotelian and other philosophical works. His observations are of a desultory character: Now he makes a beginning in one place; again, he starts afresh in another. In continually renewed approaches he endeavours to get nearer Greek thought, and to penetrate from every possible side to ancient science. He does not discard philosophy, and he does not deal conclusively with it. On a first glance, that produces a puzzling impression; but, in the sombre impulse which is upon him, the philosopher has become aware of the path he is pursuing. In searching for truth and righteousness, he is coming upon another thing, — unity and joy in his own life. In his opinion, Gazali took the matter much too easily, when he thought he could be happy only in the full possession of the truth comprehended by means of Divine illumination. In his love for the truth, which is concealed rather than revealed by the sensuous images of religious mysticism, the philosopher must be strong enough to renounce that happiness. Only pure thinking, undisturbed by any sensuous desire, is privileged to behold the supreme Godhead.

4. In his logical writings Ibn Baddja hardly departs from Farabi. Even his physical and metaphysical theories agree generally with the views of the master. But perhaps the mode, in which he represents the history of the development of the human spirit and the position of man in know-

ledge and in life, may claim a measure of interest. There
are two kinds of existence, according to his view, — one
which is moved, and one which is not moved. That which
is moved is corporeal and limited, but its everlasting movement cannot be explained by finite Body. On the contrary,
in order to explain this endless movement, an unending
power is needed, or an eternal essence, namely Spirit.
Now while the corporeal or the natural is moved from
without, and the Spirit, itself unmoved, confers movement
upon the corporeal, the Soul-substance occupies a middle
position, being that which moves itself. The relation between the natural and the psychical presents as little difficulty to Ibn Baddja as to his predecessors; but the great
problem is this: — 'How are the Soul and the Spirit related to each other, that is to say in Man?'

5. Ibn Baddja starts with the assumption that Matter
cannot exist without some Form, while Form may exist
by itself, without Matter. Otherwise, in fact, absolutely no
change is thinkable, because that is rendered possible only
by the coming and going of substantial Forms.

These Forms then, from the hylic up to the purely
spiritual, constitute a series, to which the development of
the human spirit corresponds, in so far as it realizes the
rational ideal. Man's task is to comprehend all the spiritual Forms together; first the intelligible Forms of all that
is corporeal, then the sensible-spiritual presentations of the
Soul, next the human Spirit itself and the Active Spirit
over it, and lastly the pure Spirits of the celestial spheres.
By rising through successive stages from the individual
and sensible, the presentation of which constitutes the
material on which the Spirit operates, Man attains to the

superhuman and the Divine. Now his guide in this process is Philosophy, or the knowledge of the universal, which issues from knowledge of the particular through study and reflection, aided however by the enlightening Spirit from above. Contrasted with this knowledge of the universal or the infinite, — in which Being, and becoming the object of cognition coincide, — all perception and presentation prove deceptive. Thus it is by rational knowledge, and not by religious and mystical dreaming, with the sensuous invariably clinging thereto, that the human Spirit arrives at perfection. Thinking is the highest bliss, for its very purpose is to reach all that is intelligible. But since that is the universal, the continued existence of individual human Spirits beyond this life cannot be assumed. It may be that the Soul, — which apprehends the particular in the life of sensuous-spiritual presentation, and notifies its existence in separate desires and actions, — has the faculty of continuing that existence after death, and of receiving reward or punishment; but the Spirit or the rational part of the Soul is one in all. It is only the Spirit of the entirety of Mankind, or, in other words, the one Intellect, Mind or Spirit in Humanity, — and that too in its union with the active Spirit over it, — which is eternal. This theory, which made its way into the Christendom of the Middle Ages, under the name of Averroes' Theory, is thus found even with Ibn Baddja, if not quite distinctly conceived, at all events more clearly given than with Farabi.

6. Every man does not rise to such a height of contemplation. The greater number grope about continually in the dark; they merely see the adumbrations of things, and like shadows they will pass away. Some see the Light,

it is true, and the coloured world of things, but very few
indeed recognize the essence of what they have seen. It is
only the latter, the blessed ones, who attain to life eternal, —
in which state they themselves become Light.

But now, how does the individual man get to this stage
of knowledge and blessed existence? Through action directed
by reason, and the free cultivation of his intellectual powers.
Action directed by reason is free action, that is, action in
which there is a consciousness of purpose. If one, for instance, breaks a stone to pieces, because he has stumbled
against it, he is behaving without purpose, like a child
or a lower animal; but if he does this in order that others
may not stumble against the stone, his action must be called
manlike, and directed by reason.

In order to be able to live as a man should, and to act
in a rational way, the individual man, must as far as
circumstances permit, withdraw from society. The name
borne by the Ethics of Ibn Baddja is "Guidance to the
Solitary". It demands self-culture. Generally, however, one
may avail himself of the advantages attending social life
in man, without including in the bargain its disadvantages.
The wise may associate themselves in larger or smaller
unions; such indeed is their duty, if they light upon one
another; and then they form a State within the State.
Naturally they endeavour to live in such a manner that
neither physician nor judge is necessary among them. They
grow up like plants in the open air, and do not stand in
need of the gardener's skill. They keep at a distance from
the lower enjoyments and sentiments of the multitude. They
are strangers to the movements of worldly society. And as
they are friends among themselves, this life of theirs is

wholly determined by Love. Then too as friends of God, who is the Truth, they find repose in union with the superhuman Spirit of Knowledge.

3. Ibn Tofail.

1. The sovereignty over Western Islam remained with the Berbers, but the Almohads speedily took the place of the Almoravids. Mohammed ibn Tumart, the founder of the new dynasty, had, from the year 1121, come forward as Mahdi. Under his successors Abu Yaaqub Yusuf (1163—1184) and Abu Yusuf Yaaqub (1184—1198), their sovereignty, which was centred in Marocco, reached its culminating point.

The Almohads brought with them a startling novelty in theology: The system of Ashari and Gazali, which till then had been branded as heretical, was adopted in the West. That meant an infusion of intellectualism into the teaching of the Faith, — a proceeding which could not be altogether satisfactory either to the adherents of the old Faith or to freethinkers, but which may have incited many to farther philosophizing. Hitherto an attitude of repudiation had been maintained towards all reasoning in matters of faith; and, even later, many politicians and philosophers were of opinion that the faith of the multitude should not be violently disturbed, nor elevated to knowledge, but that the provinces of Religion and of Philosophy should be kept scrupulously separate.

The Almohads were interested in questions of theology, but yet Abu Yaaqub and his successors manifested, as far as political conditions permitted, such an appreciation of secular knowledge, that philosophy was enabled to enjoy a brief period of prosperity at their court.

2. We find Abu Bekr Mohammed ibn Abdalmalik ibn
Tofail al-Qaisi (*Abubacer*) in the position of Vizir and Body-
Physician to Abu Yaaqub, after holding an appointment as
Secretary in Granada. His place of birth was the small
Andalusian town of Guadix, and he died in Marocco, the
seat of Government, in the year 1185. The life that lies
between appears to have been by no means eventful. He
was fonder of books than of men, and in his sovereign's
great library he gathered, by reading, much information
which he required for his art, or which met his ardent
thirst for knowledge. He was the *dilettante* of the philosophers of the West, and was more given to contemplative enjoyment than scientific work. Rarely did he set
himself to write. We need not perhaps put absolute faith
in his assertion that he could have fundamentally improved
the Ptolemaie system. Many Arabs made a like assertion,
without carrying it into effect.

Of Ibn Tofail's poetic ventures, one or two poems have
been preserved to us. But his principal endeavour, like
that of Ibn Sina, was to combine Greek Science and Oriental
Wisdom into a modern view of the world. That was to
him a personal concern, just as it was to Ibn Baddja. He
too occupied his mind with the relation of the individual
man to Society and its prejudices. But he went farther:
Ibn Baddja, as a rule made out the individual thinker
or a small association of independent thinkers, as constituting a State within the State, — a copy, as it were,
of the great total, or a model for happier times: Ibn Tofail
on the other hand, turned to consider the original.

3. He states the case clearly, in his work "Hai ibn
Yaqzan". The scenery is contributed by two islands, on

one of which he sets human society with its conventions, and on the other an individual man, who is being developed naturally. This society as a whole is governed by lower impulses, subjected only to some measure of outward restraint by a grossly sensuous religion. But out of this society two men, called Salaman and Asal (*Absal*, cf. IV, 4 § 7), rise to rational knowledge and control of their desires. Accomodating himself to the popular religion, the first, who is of a practical turn of mind, contrives to rule the people; but the second, being of speculative disposition and mystic leanings, wanders off to the island which lay opposite, and which he imagines to be uninhabited, — there to devote himself to study and ascetic discipline.

On that island, however, our Hai ibn Yaqzan, — *i. e.* 'the Active one, the son of the Vigilant', — had been trained into a perfect philosopher. Cast upon the island when a child, or else brought into existence there by spontaneous generation, he had been suckled by a gazelle, and then had been in the course of time left, like a Robinson Crusoe, and that entirely, to his own resources. Yet he had secured a material existence, and farther, by observation and reflection, had acquired a knowledge of Nature, the heavens, God, and his own inner being, until after seven times seven years he had attained to that which is highest, viz., the Sufi vision of God, the state of ecstasy. In this situation he was found by Asal. After they had come to understand each other, — for at first Hai was still without speech, — it was found that the philosophy of the one and the religion of the other were two forms of the same truth, except that in the first form it was somewhat less veiled. But when Hai came to know that on the opposite island an

entire people continued in darkness and error, he resolved
to proceed thither and reveal the truth to them. Here,
however, he was brought to learn by experience that the
multitude were incapable of a pure apprehension of the
truth, and that Mohammed had acted wisely in giving the
people sensuous forms instead of full light. After this result
therefore he repaired again with his friend Asal to the
uninhabited island, to serve God in spirit and in truth till
the hour of death.

4. Ibn Tofail has devoted by far the largest portion of
his romance to the course of Hai's development; but he
cannot certainly have thought that the individual man,
left to himself, is able, with the resources of Nature alone
and without the help of society, to advance so far as Hai
did. And yet his conception is perhaps rather more historical, than certain views which have been entertained
since his day, e. g. by some of the Rationalists of the
18th century. Many little touches in his work shew that
Hai was intended to represent humanity as it stands outside
of revelation. That which is accomplished in him, is the
development of Indian, Persian and Greek wisdom. One
or two hints pointing in that direction, but which cannot
be farther followed out here, may help to lend probability
to this view. Thus it is significant, to begin with, that
Hai lives on the island of Ceylon, the climate of which
was held to be such as to render spontaneous generation
possible, where also, according to the legend, Adam, the
first man, had been created, and where the Indian king
came to the Wise Man. Then Hai's first religious senti-
ment of wonder, after he had struggled up out of the
primary, animal stage, through shame and curiosity, is

elicited by fire, which has been discovered by him, — a circumstance which recalls to us the Persian religion. And his farther speculations are borrowed from Greco-Arabic Philosophy.

The affinity to Ibn Sina's Hai, which Ibn Tofail himself indicates, is clear: Only, the figure of Hai in this case presents a more human appearance. With Ibn Sina the character of Hai represents the Superhuman Spirit, but the hero of Ibn Tofail's romance seems to be the personification of the natural Spirit of Mankind illuminated from above; and that Spirit must be in accordance with the Prophet-Soul of Mohammed when rightly understood, whose utterances are to be interpreted allegorically.

Ibn Tofail has thus arrived at the same result as his Eastern predecessors. Religion must still be kept up for the ordinary man, because he cannot go beyond it. It is only a few who rise to an understanding of religious symbols; and very rarely indeed does any one attain to the unrestrained comtemplation of the highest reality. This last truth he accentuates with the greatest emphasis. Even if we do find in Hai the representative of human nature, we cannot gainsay this truth; for the representation given sets forth the supreme perfection of Man as consisting in submerging his own self in the World-Spirit, in the most lonely quietude, and withdrawn from all that is sensuous.

It is true that this condition is attained only in mature age, in which, besides, a human friend has been met with; and attention to what is material, and to the arts and sciences, forms the natural preliminary stage of spiritual perfection. Thus Ibn Tofail is permitted to look back without regret or shame upon his life spent at court.

5. We have already met frequently with the philosophical views, which Hai developed in his seven life-periods. But even his practical behaviour is specially considered by Ibn Tofail. Sufi exercises, as they are still observed among the religious orders of the East, and as they had been recommended even by Plato and the Neo-Platonists, have taken the place of the observances of religious worship enjoined by the Muslim Law. And Hai forms for himself in the seventh period of his life a system of Ethics which has a Pythagorean appearance.

Hai has set before him as the aim of his action, — to seek for the One in all things and to unite himself to the absolute and the self-existing. He sees in fact all Nature striving to reach this Highest Being. He is far above the view that everything on the earth exists for the sake of Man. Animals and plants likewise live for themselves and for God; and thus he is not permitted to deal capriciously with them. He now restricts his bodily wants to what is absolutely necessary. Ripe fruits are preferred by him, the seeds of which he piously consigns to the soil, taking anxious precaution that no kind may die out through his avidity. And only in extreme need does he touch animal food, in which case he seeks in like manner to spare the species. 'Enough for life, not enough for sleep' is his motto.

That has reference to his bodily attitude towards the earthly; but the living principle binds him to the heavens, and, like the heavens, he strives to be useful to his surroundings, and to keep his own life pure. He therefore tends the plants and protects the animals about him, in order that his island may become a paradise. He pays scrupulous attention to the cleanliness of his person and his clothing, and endeavours to give a harmonious turn to all his movements, in conformity with those of the heavenly bodies.

In this way he is gradually rendered capable of elevating his own self above earth and heaven to the pure Spirit. That is the condition of ecstasy, which no thought, no word, no image has ever been able to comprehend or express.

4. IBN ROSHD.

1. Abu-l-Walid Mohammed ibn Akhmed ibn Mohammed ibn Roshd (*Averroes*) was born at Cordova, of a family of lawyers, in the year 1126. There too he made himself master of the learned culture of his time. In 1153 he is said to have been presented to the prince Abu Yaaqub by Ibn Tofail; and we possess a report of that occurrence, full of character. After the introductory phrases of politeness the prince asked him: "What is the opinion of philosophers about the heavens? Are they eternal, or have they been brought into existence?" Ibn Roshd cautiously replied that he had not given attention to philosophy. Thereupon the prince commenced to discuss the subject with Ibn Tofail, and, to the astonishment of the listener, shewed that he was acquainted with Aristotle, Plato, and the philosophers and theologians of Islam. Then Ibn Roshd also spoke out freely, and won the favour of his high-placed master. His lot was fixed: He was destined to interpret Aristotle, as no one before him had done, that mankind might be put in complete and genuine possession of science.

He was, besides, a jurist and a physician. We find him in 1169 in the position of judge in Seville, and shortly afterwards in Cordova. Abu Yaakub, now Caliph, nominates him his Body-Physician in the year 1182; but, a short time after, he is again judge in his native city, as his father and grandfather had been. Circumstances, however, change for the worse. Philosophers are pronounced accursed, and their writings are committed to the flames. In his old age Ibn Roshd is banished by Abu Yusuf to Elisana (Lucena, near Cordova), but yet he dies in Marocco the capital, on the 10th December, 1198.

2. It was upon Aristotle that his activity was concentrated. All that he could procure of that philosopher's works, or about them, he subjected to diligent study and careful comparison. Writings of the Greeks, which are now lost either entirely or in part, were still known to Ibn Roshd in translated form. He goes critically and systematically to work: He paraphrases Aristotle and he interprets him, now with comparative brevity, and anon in greater detail, both in moderate-sized and in bulky commentaries. He thus merits the name of "the Commentator", which also is assigned to him in Dante's "Commedia" [1]. It looks as if the Philosophy of the Muslims had been fated in him to come to an understanding of Aristotle, just that it might then expire, after that end had been attained. Aristotle for him is the supremely perfect man, the greatest thinker, the philosopher who was in possession of an infallible truth. New discoveries in Astronomy, Art or Physics could make no alteration in that respect. Of course it is possible to misunderstand Aristotle: Ibn Roshd himself came to have a different and better understanding of many a point which he took from the works of Farabi and Ibn Sina; but yet he lived con-

[1] "Averrois, che'l gran comento feo" Canto IV.

tinually in the belief that Aristotle, when rightly understood, corresponds to the highest knowledge which is attainable by man. In the eternal revolution of worldly events Aristotle has reached a height which it is impossible to transcend. Men who have come after him are frequently put to the cost of much trouble and reflection to deduce the views which readily disclosed themselves to the first master. Gradually, however, all doubt and contradiction are reduced to silence, for Aristotle is one who is more than man, destined as it were by Providence to illustrate how far the human race is capable of advancing in its approximation to the World-Spirit. As being the sublimest incarnation of the Spirit of Mankind, Ibn Roshd would like to call his master the 'Divine' Teacher.

It will be shewn by what follows, that even in the instance of Ibn Roshd, unmeasured admiration for Aristotle did not suffice to bring about a perfect comprehension of his thoughts. He allows no opportunity to pass of doing battle with Ibn Sina, and, upon occasion, he parts company with Farabi and Ibn Baddja, — men to whom he owes a great deal. He carps at all his predecessors, in a far more disagreeable fashion than Aristotle did in the case of his teacher Plato. And yet he himself is far from having got beyond the interpretation of Neo-Platonic expositors and the misconceptions of Syrian and Arab translators. Frequently he follows even the superficial Themistius in opposition to the judicious Alexander of Aphrodisias, or else he tries to combine their views.

3. Ibn Roshd is above all a fanatical admirer of the Aristotelian Logic. Without it one cannot be happy, and it is a pity that Plato and Socrates were ignorant of it!

The happiness of men is measured by the degree of their logical attainments. With the discernment of a critic he recognizes Porphyry's "Isagoge" as superfluous, but he still counts the "Rhetoric" and the "Poetics" as forming part of the Organon. And then the oddest misapprehensions are met with. For example, Tragedy and Comedy are turned into Panegyrics and Lampoons; poetical probability has to be content with signifying either truth capable of demonstration, or deceptive appearance; recognition on the stage (ἀναγνώρισις) becomes Apodictic judgment, and so on. Of course he has absolutely no conception of the Greek world; and that is venial, for he could not have had any notion of it. And yet we do not readily excuse one who has been so severe a critic of others.

Like his predecessors, Ibn Roshd lays especial emphasis upon Grammar, as far as it is common to all languages. This common principle, and therefore the universal one, Aristotle, he thinks, keeps always before him in his Hermeneutics, and even in the Rhetoric. Accordingly the Arab philosopher is also bound to adhere to it, although in illustrating universal rules he may take his examples from the Arabic language and literature. But it is universal rules which form his object, for science is the knowledge of the universal.

Logic smooths the path for the ascent of our cognition from sensuous particularity to pure rational truth. The multitude will always live in the sensuous element, groping about in error. Defective mental parts and poor education, and depraved habits to boot, prevent them from making any advance. But still it must be within the power of some to arrive at a knowledge of truth. The eagle looks the sun in the face, for if no being could look at him, Nature would have made something in vain. Whatever shines there is meant to be seen; and so whatever exists is meant to be known, were it only by one single man. Now truth exists; and the love for it which fills our hearts would have been all in vain, if we could not approach it. Ibn Roshd thinks that he has come to know the truth in the case of many things, and even that he has been able to discover absolute Truth. He would not, with Lessing, have cared to resign himself to a mere search for it.

Truth, in fact, has been given him in Aristotle; and from that standpoint he looks down upon Muslim theology. Certainly he recognizes that religion has a truth of its own, but theology is repugnant to him. It wants to prove what cannot be proved in this way. Revelation, as contained in the Koran, — according to the teaching of Ibn Roshd and others, and similarly of Spinoza in later times, — does not aim at making men learned, but at making them better. Not knowledge, but obedience or moral practice is the aim of the lawgiver, who knows that human welfare can only be realized in society.

4. That which especially distinguishes Ibn Roshd from those who preceded him, and in particular from Ibn Sina, is the unequivocal mode in which he conceives of the world as an eternal process of 'becoming'. The world as a whole is an eternally necessary unity, without any possibility of non-existence or of different existence. Matter and Form can only be separated in thought. Forms do not wander like ghosts through dull Matter, but are contained in it after the manner of germs. The Material Forms, in the guise of natural forces, operate in an eternal process

of generation, never separated from matter, but yet deserving
to be called divine. Absolute origination or extinction there
is none, for all happening is a transition from potentiality to actuality, and from actuality back to potentiality,
in which process like is ever generated by like and by
that alone.

But there is a graded order in the world of Being.
The material or substantial Form stands midway between
mere Accident and pure (or separate) Form. Substantial
Forms also exhibit varieties of degree, — intermediate
conditions between potentiality and actuality. And, finally,
the whole system of Forms, from the nethermost hylic
Form up to the Divine Essence, the original Form of the
whole, constitutes one compact structure rising tier upon tier.

Now the eternal process of Becoming, within the given
System, presupposes an eternal movement, and that again
an eternal Mover. If the world had had an origin, we might
have reasoned from it to another and a similarly originated
corporeal world, which had produced it, and so on without
end. If again it had been a 'possible' entity, we might have
inferred a 'possible' entity out of which it had proceeded,
and so on *ad infinitum*. And according to Ibn Roshd, it
is only the hypothesis of a world moved as a unity and of
eternal necessity, that yields us the possibility of inferring
a Being, separate from the world, yet eternally moving
it, who in his continually producing that movement and
maintaining the fair order of the All, may legitimately
be called the Author of the world, and who in the Spirits
that move the Spheres, — for every separate kind of movement demands its separate principle, — possesses agents
to give effect to his activity.

The essence of the First Mover, or of God, as well as of the Sphere-Spirits, is found by Ibn Roshd in Thought, in which unity of Being is given him. Thought which is identical with its object is the sole positive definition of the Divine Essence; but Being and Unity absolutely synchronize with such Thought. In other words, Being and Unity are not annexed to the Essence, but are given only in Thought, just like all universals. Thought produces everywhere the general in the particular. It is true that the universal as a disposition is operative in things, but the universal *qua* universal exists in the understanding alone. Or, in possibility (or potentiality) it exists in things, but it exists actually in the understanding, — that is, it has more Being, — a higher kind of existence, — in the understanding than in things.

If now the question is asked, — 'Does Divine Thought take in merely the general, or does it take in the particular too?', Ibn Roshd replies, 'It does not directly take in either the one or the other, for the Divine Essence transcends both of them. Divine Thought produces the All and embraces the All. God is the principle, the original Form, and the final aim of all things. He is the order of the world, the reconciliation of all opposites, the All itself in its highest mode of existence. It follows of course from this theory, that there can be no talk of a Divine Providence in the ordinary sense of the term.

5. Two kinds of Being we know: one which is moved, and one which causes motion, though itself unmoved, — or a corporeal and a spiritual. But it is in the spiritual that the higher unity or perfection of all Being lies, and that too in graded order. It is thus no abstract unity. The farther the

Sphere-Spirits are from the First, so much the less simple
are they. All know themselves, but in their knowledge there
is at the same time a reference to the First Cause. The
result is a kind of parallelism between the corporeal and
the spiritual. There is something in the lower Spirits which
corresponds to the composition of the corporeal out of
Matter and Form. What is mingled with the purely spiritual is of course no mere Matter, that could suffer anything, but yet it is something resembling Matter, —
something which has the faculty of taking to itself something else. Otherwise the multiplicity of *intelligibilia* could
not be brought into harmony with the unity of the Spirit
which apprehends them.

Matter suffers, but Spirit receives. This parallelism, with
its subtle distinction, has been introduced by Ibn Roshd
with special reference to the human Spirit.

6. Ibn Roshd is firmly of opinion that the human soul
is related to its body, as Form is to Matter. He is completely in earnest on this point. The theory of numerous
immortal souls he most decidedly rejects, combating Ibn
Sina. The soul has an existence only as a completion of
the body with which it is associated.

As regards empirical psychology he has anxiously endeavoured to keep by Aristotle, in opposition to Galen and
others; but in the doctrine of the *"nous"* he diverges from
his master not inconsiderably, without being aware of it.
His conception, — springing from Neo-Platonic views, —
of the Material Reason, is peculiar. It is not a mere ap-
titude or capacity of the human soul, neither is it equivalent to the sensuous-spiritual life of presentation, but
it is something above the soul, and above the indivi-

dual. The Material Reason is eternal, imperishable Spirit, as eternal and imperishable as the pure Reason or the Active Spirit over us. The ascription of a separate existence to Matter in the domain of the corporeal, is here transferred by Ibn Roshd, — following of course Themistius and others, — to the region of the spiritual.

The Material Reason is thus eternal substance. The natural aptitudes, or the capacity of the human individual for intellectual knowledge Ibn Roshd denominates the Passive Reason. That comes into being and disappears, with men as individuals, but the Material Reason is eternal, like Man as a race.

But a measure of obscurity remains, and it could hardly have been otherwise, about the relation between the Active Spirit and the Receptive Spirit, (if we may for the time use this last term for the Material Reason). The Active Spirit renders intelligible the presentations of the human soul, while the Receptive Spirit absorbs these *intelligibilia*. The life of the soul in individual men thus forms the meeting-place of this mystic pair of lovers. And such places differ very greatly. It depends on the entire capacity of a man's soul, and on the disposition of his perceptions, in what degree the Active Spirit can elevate these to intelligibility, and how far the Receptive Spirit is in a position to make them a portion of its own contents. This explains why men are not all at the same stage of spiritual knowledge. But the sum of spiritual knowledge in the world continues unaltered, although the partition of it undergoes individual variations. By a necessity of nature, the Philosopher re-appears, without fail, whether an Aristotle or an Ibn Roshd, in whose brain Being becomes Idea. It is true that the thoughts of individual men occur in the element of time, and that the Receptive Spirit is changeable, so far as the individual has a part in it; but considered as the Reason of the Human Race, that Spirit is eternally incapable of change, like the Active Spirit from the last Sphere above us.

7. On the whole, three great heresies set the system of Ibn Roshd in opposition to the theology of the three world-religions of his time: first, the eternity of the material world and of the Spirits that move it; next, the necessary causal nexus in all that happens in the world, so that no place is left for providence, miracle, and the like; and, thirdly, the perishable nature of all that is individual, by which theory individual immortality is also taken away.

Considered logically the assumption of a number of independent Sphere-Spirits under God does not appear to have any sufficient basis. But Ibn Roshd, like his predecessors, gets over this difficulty by asserting that these Sphere-Spirits do not differ individually but only in kind. Their sole purpose was to explain the different movements in the system of the world, so long as its unity was still unknown. After the Ptolemaic system of the world had been put aside, and these intermediary Spirits had become superfluous, men identified the Active Spirit with God, as, for the matter of that, they had even in earlier times attempted to do, on speculative and religious grounds. It was merely one step farther, to identify even the eternal Spirit of Man with God. Ibn Roshd did neither of these things, at least according to the strict letter of his writings; but his system, when consistently carried out, made

‚ it possible to take these steps, and in this way to arrive generally at a Pantheistic conception of the world. On the other hand Materialism might easily find support in the system, however decidedly our philosopher contended against such a view; for where the eternity, form and efficacy of all that is material are so strongly emphasized, as was done by him, Spirit may indeed still receive the name of king, but seemingly by the favour merely of the material.

Ibn Roshd deserves at all events to be called a bold and consistent thinker, although not an original one. Theoretical philosophy was sufficient for him; but yet he owed it to his time and his position to come to an understanding with religion and practice. We may devote a few words to this point.

8. Ibn Roshd often takes the opportunity of expressing himself against the -uneducated rulers and obscurantist theologians of his own day; but he continues to prefer life as a citizen to a solitary life. He even thanks his opponents for many a piece of instruction, — and that is a pleasing touch of character. He thinks that the solitary life produces no arts or sciences, and that one can at the most enjoy in it what has been gained already, or perhaps improve it a little. But every one should contribute to the weal of the whole community: even women as well as men should be of service to society and the State. In this opinion Ibn Roshd agrees with Plato (for he was not acquainted with the Politics of Aristotle), and he remarks with entire good sense that a great deal of the poverty and distress of his time arises from the circumstance that women are kept like domestic animals or house plants for purposes of gratification, of a very questionable

character besides, instead of being allowed to take part in the production of material and intellectual wealth, and in the preservation of the same.

In his Ethical system our philosopher animadverts with great severity upon the doctrine of the professors of Law, that a thing is good or bad only because God so willed it. On the contrary, says he, everything has its moral character from nature or in conformity with reason. The action which is determined by rational discernment is moral. It is not, of course, the individual Reason, but the Reason which looks to the welfare of the community or State, to which appeal must be made in the last instance.

Ibn Roshd regards religion also from a statesman's point of view. He values it on account of its moral purpose. It is Law, not Learning. He is therefore constantly engaged in fighting the Theologians, who wish to understand intellectually, instead of obeying with docile faith. He makes it a reproach to Gazali, that he has allowed philosophy to exercise an influence upon his religious doctrine, and thereby has led many into doubt and unbelief. The people should believe, exactly in accordance with what stands in the Book. That is Truth, — Truth meant no doubt for a bigger sort of children, to whom we convey it in the form of stories. Whatever goes beyond this, comes of evil. For example, the Koran has two proofs of the existence of God, which are evident to every one, viz: the Divine care of everything, especially of human beings, — and the production of life in plants, animals, &c. These deliverances should not be disturbed, nor should the literal acceptation of revelation be quibbled about, in the theological fashion. For, the proofs which theologians adduce

of the existence of God can make no stand against a
scientific criticism, any more than the proof which is furnished from the notion of the possible and the necessary,
in Farabi and Ibn Sina. All this leads to Atheism and
Libertinism. In the interests of morality, and therefore of
the State, this semi-theology should be fought against.

On the other hand, philosophers who have attained
to knowledge are permitted to interpret the Word of God
in the Koran. In the light of the highest truth they understand what is aimed at therein; and they tell merely just
so much of it to the ordinary man as he is capable of
apprehending. In this way the most admirable harmony
results. Religious precept and philosophy are in agreement
with one another, precisely because they are not seeking
the same thing. They are related as practice and theory.
In the philosopher's conception of religion, he allows its
validity in its own domain, so that philosophy by no means
rejects religion. Philosophy, however, is the highest form
of truth, and at the same time the most sublime religion. The religion of the philosopher, in fact, is the knowledge of all that exists.

But yet this view has the appearance of being irreligious;
and a positive religion can never be content to recognize
the leading position of philosophy in the realm of truth.
It was only natural that the theologians of the West, like
their brethren of the East should seek to profit by the
favour of circumstances, and take no rest until they had
reduced the mistress to the position of the handmaid of
Theology.

VII. CONCLUSION.

1. Ibn Khaldun.

1. The Philosophy of Ibn Roshd, and his interpretation of Aristotle, have had extremely little effect upon the Muslim world. Many of his works, in the original, are lost, and we have them only in Hebrew and Latin translations. He had no disciples or followers. In retired corners no doubt many a free-thinker or Mystic might be met with, to whose mind it looked sufficiently fantastic to toil earnestly with philosophic questions of a theoretical kind; but Philosophy was not permitted to influence general culture or the condition of affairs. Before the victorious arms of the Christians the material civilization as well as the intellectual culture of the Muslims retreated farther and farther. Spain became like Africa, where the Berber was ruler. The times were serious: the very existence of Islam in these regions was at stake. Men made ready for fighting against the enemy, or even against one another; and pious brethren every'where formed unions for mystic observances. In the Sufi orders of these people, a few philosophical formulae at least were still preserved in safety. When, towards the middle of the thirteenth

century, the emperor Frederick II submitted a number
of philosophical questions to the Muslim scholars of Ceuta,
the Almohad Abdalwahid charged Ibn Sabin, founder of
a Mystic order, to reply to them. He did so, drawling
forth in a pedantic tone the views both of ancient and
recent philosophers, and affording a glimpse of the Sufi
secret, — that God is the reality of all things. The only
thing, however, which we can learn from his answers, may
be said to be, that Ibn Sabin had read books, of which
he thought the Emperor Frederick had not the faintest
notion.

2. In small State-systems, the Muslim civilization of
the West drifted away, now rising, now falling. But before it vanished completely, a man appeared, who endeavoured to discover the law of its formation, and who thought
to found therewith a new philosophical discipline, — the
Philosophy of Society or of History. That remarkable man
was Ibn Khaldûn, born at Tunis is the year 1332, of a
family belonging to Seville. There he also received his upbringing, and there he was next instructed in philosophy,
partly by a teacher who had been trained in the East.
After studying all known sciences, he occupied himself
sometimes in the service of the Government, and sometimes in travel, proving everywhere an excellent observer.
He served various princes in the capacity of secretary,
and he was ambassador at several courts in Spain and
Africa: as such he visited the Christian court of Peter
the Cruel in Seville. He was also at the court of Tamer-
lane in Damascus. He had thus acquired a wide and full
experience of the world, when he died at Cairo in the
year 1406.

In character perhaps he does not take a high rank; but a measure of vanity, dilettantism and the like, may readily be forgiven to the man who, above all others in his time, lived for Science.

3. Ibn Khaldûn was not satisfied with the School-Philosophy, as he had come to know it. His picture of the world would not fit its conventional framing. If he had been somewhat more given to theorizing, he might no doubt have constructed a system of Nominalism. Philosophers pretend to know everything; but the universe seems to him too great to be capable of being comprehended by our understanding. There are more beings and things, infinitely more, than Man can ever know. "God creates what you know nothing of". Logical deductions frequently do not agree with the empirical world of individual things, which becomes known by observation alone. That we can reach truth by merely applying the rules of Logic, is a vain imagination: therefore reflection on what is given in experience is the task of the scientific man. And he must not rest satisfied with his own individual experience; but, with critical care he must draw upon the sum of the collected experience of mankind, which has been handed down.

By nature the soul is devoid of knowledge; but yet by nature it has the power of reflecting on the experience which is given, and elaborating it. In the course of such reflection, there frequently springs forth, as if by inspiration, the proper middle term, by means of which the insight which has been gained may be arranged and explained according to the rules of Formal Logic. Logic does not produce knowledge: it merely traces the path which our reflection ought to take: it points out how we arrive at knowledge; and it has the farther value of being able to preserve us from error, and to sharpen the intellect and keep it to accuracy in thinking. It is therefore an auxiliary science, and ought to be cultivated even for its own sake by one or two qualified men, called specially to that task; but it does not possess the fundamental importance which is attributed to it by the Philosophers. The path which it indicates for our reflection to take, is at need followed by scientific talent in any individual science, quite independently of logical guidance.

Ibn Khaldûn is a sober thinker. He combats Alchemy and Astrology on rational grounds. To the Mystic rationalism of the Philosophers he opposes frequently the simple doctrines of his religion, whether from personal conviction, or from political considerations. But religion exercises no greater influence upon his scientific opinions than Neo-Platonic Aristotelianism. Plato's Republic, the Pythagorean-Platonic Philosophy, but without its marvel-mongering outgrowths, and the historical works of his oriental fore-runners, particularly of Masudi, have had most influence on the development of his thoughts.

4. Ibn Khaldûn comes forward with a claim to establish a new philosophical discipline, of which Aristotle had no conception. Philosophy is the science of what exists, developed from its own principles or reasons. But what the Philosophers advance, about the high Spirit-world and the Divine Essence, does not correspond thereto: that which they say on these subjects is incapable of proof. We know our world of men much better; and a more certain deliverance may be given regarding it, by means of obser-

vation and inner mental experience. Here facts permit of
being authenticated, and their causes discovered. Now, so
far as the latter process is feasible in History, *i. e.* so far
as historical events are capable of being traced back to
their causes, and historical laws capable of being discovered,
History deserves actually to be called Science and a part
of Philosophy. Thus the idea of History as Science clearly
emerges. It has nothing to do with curiosity, frivolousness,
general benefit, edifying effect &c. It should, although in
the service of the higher purposes of life, determine nothing
except facts, endeavouring to find out their causal nexus.
The work must be done in a critical, unprejudiced spirit.
The governing principle which rules here is this, — that
the cause corresponds to the effect, — that is to say,
that like events presuppose the same conditions, or, that
under the same circumstances of civilization the like events
will occur. Now, as it is a probable assumption that the
nature of men and of society undergoes no change by the
advance of time, or no considerable change, a living comprehension of the present is the best means of investigating the past. That which is fully known and is under
our very eyes permits us to form retrospective conclusions
in regard to the less fully known events of an earlier time:
it promises even a glance into the future. In every instance, therefore, tradition must be tested by the present;
and if it tells us of things which are impossible now, we
must for that very reason doubt its truth. Past and Present are as like one another as two drops of water. If
understood absolutely, that might have been said even by
Ibn Roshd. But according to Ibn Khaldûn it is only quite
generally valid as a principle of research. In detail it

suffers many a limitation; and in any case it has itself
to be established by facts.

5. What then is the subject of History as a philosophical discipline? Ibn Khaldûn answers that it is the Social
life, — the collective, material and intellectual culture of
Society. History has to show how men work and provide
themselves with food, why they contend with each other
and associate in larger communities under single leaders,
how at last they find in a settled life leisure for the cultivation of the higher arts and sciences, how a finer culture
comes into bloom in this way out of rude beginnings, and
how again this in time dies away.

The forms of Society which replace one another are, in
the opinion of Ibn Khaldûn; 1) Society in the Nomad
condition; 2) Society under a Military Dynasty; and
3) Society after the City type. The first question is that
of food. Men and nations are differentiated by their eco-
nomical position, as nomads, settled herdsmen, agricul-
turists. Want leads to rapine and war, and to subjection
to a monarch who will lead them. Thus dynastic authority is developed. This again founds for itself a city, where
division of labour or mutual assistance produces prosperity.
But this prosperity leads to degenerate idleness and luxury.
Labour has in the first place brought about prosperity; but
now, at the highest stage of civilization, men get others to
labour for them, and often without any direct equivalent,
because regard or even servility to the upper classes, and
extortionate treatment of the lower, secure success. But,
all the same, men are coming to depend upon others.
Needs are always growing more clamant, and taxes more
oppressive. Rich spendthrifts and tax-payers grow poor, and

their unnatural life makes them ill and miserable. [1] The old warlike customs have been refined away, so that people are no longer capable of defending themselves. The bond, — formed by a sense of belonging to one community, or the bond of Religion, — by the help of which the necessity and the will of the chief knit the individual members together in older days, is relaxed, for the citizens are not pious. Everything, therefore, is ready to break up from within. And then appears a new and powerful nomad race from the desert, or a people not so greatly over-civilized, but possessed of a firmer public spirit; and it falls upon the effeminate city. Thereafter a new State is formed, which appropriates the material and intellectual wealth of the old culture, and the same history is repeated. It fares with States and the larger associations of men, just as with single families: their history is brought to a close, in from three to six generations. The first generation founds; the second maintains, as perhaps the third or even farther generations also do; the last demolishes. That is the cycle of all civilization.

6. According to August Müller the theory of Ibn Khaldûn is in conformity with the history of Spain, West Africa and Sicily, from the eleventh to the fifteenth century, — from the study of which, in fact, it was taken. His own historical work is a compilation, it is true. In detail he is often at fault, when he criticizes tradition with the help of his theory; but there is an abundance of fine psycho-

---

[1] Ibn Khaldûn speaks only of rich people who have grown poor, and says nothing of the misery of the proletariate, and that which prevails in large cities, as we know it. He lived too in smaller cities, for the most part, and till late in life admired Cairo from a distance.

logical and political observation in his philosophical Introduction, and as a whole it is a masterly performance.
The ancients never dealt thoroughly with the problem of
History. They have bequeathed to us great works of art
in their historical compositions, but no philosophical establishment of History as a Science. That mankind, though
existing from all eternity, long failed to attain to much of
the higher civilization, was explained by elementary occurrences, such as earthquakes, floods, and the like. On the
other hand Christian philosophy regarded History with its
vicissitudes as the realization of, or the preparation for,
the kingdom of God upon the earth. Now Ibn Khaldûn
was the first to endeavour, — with full consciousness and
in a statement amply substantiated, — to derive the development of human society from proximate causes. The
conditions of race, climate, production of commodities,
and so on, are discussed, and are set forth in their effect
upon the sensuous and intellectual constitution of man and
of society. In the course which is run by civilization he
finds an intimate conformity to Law. He searches everywhere for natural causes, with the utmost completeness
which was possible for him. He also asserts his belief that
the chain of causes and effects reaches its conclusion in
an Ultimate Cause. The series cannot go on without end,
and therefore we argue that there is a God. But this deduction, as he calls it, properly means this, — that we
are not in a position to become acquainted with all things
and the manner of their operation: it is virtually a confession of our ignorance. Conscious ignorance is even a
kind of knowledge; but knowledge should be pursued, as
far as possible. In clearing the way for his new science,

Ibn Khaldûn considers that he has merely indicated the main problems, and merely suggested generally the method and the subject of the science. But he hopes that others will come after him to carry on his investigations and propound fresh problems, with sound understanding and sure knowledge.

Ibn Khaldûn's hope has been realized, but not in Islam. As he was without forerunners, he remained without successors. But yet his work has been of lasting influence in the East. Many Muslim statesmen who, from the fifteenth century onwards, drove so many a European sovereign or diplomatist to despair, had studied in our philosopher's school.

2. The Arabs and Scholasticism.

1. To the victor belongs the bride. In the wars which were waged in Spain between Christians and Muslims, the former had often come under the influence of the attractions of Moorish fair ones. Many a Christian knight had celebrated "the nine-days' religious rite" with a Moorish woman. But besides material wealth and sensual enjoyment, the charm of intellectual culture had also its effect upon the conqueror. And Arab Science thus presented the appearance of a lovely bride to the eyes of many men who felt their want of knowledge.

It was the Jews especially who played the part of matchmakers in the transaction. The Jews had participated in all the transformations of Muslim intellectual culture: many of them wrote in Arabic, and others translated Arabic writings into Hebrew; not a few philosophical works by Muslim authors owe their preservation to the latter circumstance.

The development of this Jewish study of philosophy culminated in Maimonides (1135—1204), who sought, chiefly under the influence of Farabi and Ibn Sina, to reconcile Aristotle with the Old Testament. In part he expounded the doctrines of philosophy from the text of revelation, and in part he restricted the Aristotelian philosophy to what belongs to this earth, while a knowledge of that which is above it, had to be gained from the Word of God.

In the various Muslim States, at the time when they were most flourishing, the Jews had shewn an interest in scientific work, and they had not only been tolerated, but even regarded with favour. Their position, however, was altered, when those States were together overthrown, and when the decline of their civilization ensued. Expelled by fanatical mobs they fled for refuge to Christian lands, and particularly to Southern France, there to fulfil their mission as the disseminators of culture.

2. The Muslim world and the Christian world of the West came into contact at two points, — in Lower Italy and in Spain. At the court of the Emperor Frederick II in Palermo, Arab science was eagerly cultivated and made accessible to Latinists. The Emperor and his son Manfred presented the Universities of Bologna and Paris with translations of philosophical works, partly rendered from the Arabic, and partly direct from the Greek.

Of much greater importance and influence, however, was the activity of translators in Spain. In Toledo, which had been re-captured by the Christians, there existed a rich Arabic Mosque-library, the renown of which, as a centre of culture, had penetrated far into the Christian countries of the North. Arabs of mixed lineage and Jews, some of them converts to Christianity, worked together there, along with Spanish Christians. Fellow-workers were present from all countries. Thus co-operated as translators, for example, Johannes Hispanus and Gundisalinus (first half of the twelfth century), Gerard of Cremona (1114—1187), Michael the Scot and Hermann the German (between 1240 and 1246). We are not yet in possession of sufficiently detailed information regarding the labours of these men. Their translations may be called faithful, to the extent that every word in the Arabic original, or the Hebrew (or Spanish?) version has some Latin word corresponding to it; but they are not generally distinguished by an intelligent appreciation of the subject matter. To understand these translations thoroughly is a difficult thing, for one who is not conversant with Arabic. Many Arabic words which were taken over as they stood, and many proper names, disfigured beyond recognition, flit about with the air of ghosts. All this may well have produced sad confusion in the brains of Latinist students of Philosophy; and the thoughts, which were being disclosed afresh, had themselves at least an equally perplexing tendency.

The activity of translators kept pace generally with the interest shewn by Christian circles, and this interest followed a development similar to that which we had occasion to observe in Eastern and Western Islam (cf. VI, 1 § 2). The earliest translations were those of works on Mathematical Astrology, Medicine, Natural Philosophy, and Psychology, including Logical and Metaphysical material. As time went on, people restricted themselves more to Aristotle and commentaries upon him; but, at first, a

preference was shewn for everything that met the craving
for the marvellous.

Kindi became known chiefly as a physician and an astrologer. Ibn Sina produced a notable effect by his 'Medicine',
and his empirical psychology, and also by his Natural
Philosophy and his Metaphysics. Compared with him, Farabi
and Ibn Baddja exercised a less considerable influence.
Lastly came the Commentaries of Ibn Roshd (*Averroes*);
and the reputation which they gained, along with that
which was secured by Ibn Sina's Canon of Medicine, has
been longest maintained.

3. What then does the Christian Philosophy of the
Middle Ages owe to the Muslims? The answer to this
question lies properly outside the scope of the present
monograph. It is a special task, which necessitates the ran-
sacking of many folios, none of which I have read. In
general terms it may be affirmed that in the translations
from the Arabic a twofold novelty was disclosed to the
Christian West. In the first place men came to possess
Aristotle, both in his Logic and in his Physics and Metaphysics, more completely than they had hitherto known
him. But still this circumstance was only of passing importance, though stimulating for the moment, for erelong
all his writings were translated much more accurately,
direct from the Greek into Latin. The most important
result, however, was — that from the writings of the
Arabs, particularly of Ibn Roshd, a peculiar conception
of the Aristotelian doctrines, as constituting the highest
truth, came to the knowledge of men. This was bound
to give occasion for contradiction, or for compromise, between theology and philosophy, or even for denial of the

Church's creed. Thus the influence of Muslim Philosophy
upon the scholastic development of Church dogma was
partly of a stimulating, partly of a disintegrating character;
for, in the Christian world, philosophy and theology were
not yet able to proceed side by side in an attitude of
mutual indifference, as doubtless happened in the case of
Muslim thinkers. Christian Dogmatic had adopted too
much Greek Philosophy already in the first centuries of its
development, to admit of such an attitude: it could even
assimilate a little more. It was therefore relatively easier
to get the better of the simple teachings of Islam than
the complicated dogmas of Christianity.

In the twelfth century, when the influence of the Arabs
commenced to operate in that field, Christian Theology
exhibited a Neo-Platonic, Augustinian character. That
character continued to be kept up with the Franciscans,
even in the thirteenth century. Now the Pythagorean-
Platonic tendency, in Muslim thought, harmonized well with
this. Ibn Gebirol (*Avencebrol*, v. VI, 1 § 2) was, for Duns
Scotus, an authority of the first rank. On the other hand,
the great Dominicans, Albert and Thomas, who decided
the future of the doctrine of the Church, adopted a modified Aristotelianism, with which a good deal out of Farabi,
but especially out of Ibn Sina and Maimonides, agreed
quite well.

A more profound influence emanates from Ibn Roshd,
but not till about the middle of the thirteenth century,
and, in fact, in Paris, the centre of the Christian scientific
education of that time. In the year 1256 Albertus Magnus
writes against Averroes; and fifteen years later Thomas
Aquinas controverts the Averroists. Their leader is Siger

of Brabant (known from 1266), member of the Parisian
Faculty of Arts. He does not shrink from the rigorous,
logical results of the Averroist system. And just as Ibn
Roshd censures Ibn Sina, so Siger criticizes the great Albert
and the saintly Thomas, although in terms of the utmost
respect. It is true that he asseverates his submission to
Revelation; but still, his reason confirms what Aristotle,
— as he is expounded, in doubtful cases, by Ibn Roshd, —
has taught in his works. This subtle intellectualism of his,
however, does not please the theologians. At the instance
of the Franciscans, it would seem, who perhaps wished
also to strike at the Aristotelianism of the Dominicans,
he was persecuted by the Inquisition, till he died
in prison at Orvieto (*circa* 1281—1284). Dante, who
possibly knew nothing of his heresies has placed Siger in
Paradise as the representative of secular wisdom. The
two champions of Muslim Philosophy, on the other hand,
he met with in the vestibule of the Inferno, in the company of the great and wise men of Greece and Rome.
Ibn Sina and Ibn Roshd there end the series of the
great men of heathendom, towards whom succeeding ages,
like Dante, have so often lifted up their eyes in admiration.

INDEX OF PERSONAL NAMES.

A CATALOGUE OF SELECTED DOVER BOOKS
IN ALL FIELDS OF INTEREST

A CATALOGUE OF SELECTED DOVER BOOKS
IN ALL FIELDS OF INTEREST

AMERICA'S OLD MASTERS, James T. Flexner. Four men emerged unexpectedly from provincial 18th century America to leadership in European art: Benjamin West, J. S. Copley, C. R. Peale, Gilbert Stuart. Brilliant coverage of lives and contributions. Revised, 1967 edition. 69 plates. 365pp. of text.
21806-6 Paperbound $3.00

FIRST FLOWERS OF OUR WILDERNESS: AMERICAN PAINTING, THE COLONIAL PERIOD, James T. Flexner. Painters, and regional painting traditions from earliest Colonial times up to the emergence of Copley, West and Peale Sr., Foster, Gustavus Hesselius, Feke, John Smibert and many anonymous painters in the primitive manner. Engaging presentation, with 162 illustrations. xxii + 368pp.
22180-6 Paperbound $3.50

THE LIGHT OF DISTANT SKIES: AMERICAN PAINTING, 1760-1835, James T. Flexner. The great generation of early American painters goes to Europe to learn and to teach: West, Copley, Gilbert Stuart and others. Allston, Trumbull, Morse; also contemporary American painters—primitives, derivatives, academics—who remained in America. 102 illustrations. xiii + 306pp. 22179-2 Paperbound $3.00

A HISTORY OF THE RISE AND PROGRESS OF THE ARTS OF DESIGN IN THE UNITED STATES, William Dunlap. Much the richest mine of information on early American painters, sculptors, architects, engravers, miniaturists, etc. The only source of information for scores of artists, the major primary source for many others. Unabridged reprint of rare original 1834 edition, with new introduction by James T. Flexner, and 394 new illustrations. Edited by Rita Weiss. 6⅝ x 9⅝.
21695-0, 21696-9, 21697-7 Three volumes, Paperbound $13.50

EPOCHS OF CHINESE AND JAPANESE ART, Ernest F. Fenollosa. From primitive Chinese art to the 20th century, thorough history, explanation of every important art period and form, including Japanese woodcuts; main stress on China and Japan, but Tibet, Korea also included. Still unexcelled for its detailed, rich coverage of cultural background, aesthetic elements, diffusion studies, particularly of the historical period. 2nd, 1913 edition. 242 illustrations. lii + 439pp. of text.
20364-6, 20365-4 Two volumes, Paperbound $6.00

THE GENTLE ART OF MAKING ENEMIES, James A. M. Whistler. Greatest wit of his day deflates Oscar Wilde, Ruskin, Swinburne; strikes back at inane critics, exhibitions, art journalism; aesthetics of impressionist revolution in most striking form. Highly readable classic by great painter. Reproduction of edition designed by Whistler. Introduction by Alfred Werner. xxxvi + 334pp.
21875-9 Paperbound $2.50

INCIDENTS OF TRAVEL IN YUCATAN, John L. Stephens. Classic (1843) exploration of jungles of Yucatan, looking for evidences of Maya civilization. Stephens found many ruins; comments on travel adventures, Mexican and Indian culture. 127 striking illustrations by F. Catherwood. Total of 669 pp.
20926-1, 20927-X Two volumes, Paperbound $5.00

INCIDENTS OF TRAVEL IN CENTRAL AMERICA, CHIAPAS, AND YUCATAN, John L. Stephens. An exciting travel journal and an important classic of archeology. Narrative relates his almost single-handed discovery of the Mayan culture, and exploration of the ruined cities of Copan, Palenque, Utatlan and others; the monuments they dug from the earth, the temples buried in the jungle, the customs of poverty-stricken Indians living a stone's throw from the ruined palaces. 115 drawings by F. Catherwood. Portrait of Stephens. xii + 812pp.
22404-X, 22405-8 Two volumes, Paperbound $6.00

A NEW VOYAGE ROUND THE WORLD, William Dampier. Late 17-century naturalist joined the pirates of the Spanish Main to gather information; remarkably vivid account of buccaneers, pirates; detailed, accurate account of botany, zoology, ethnography of lands visited. Probably the most important early English voyage, enormous implications for British exploration, trade, colonial policy. Also most interesting reading. Argonaut edition, introduction by Sir Albert Gray. New introduction by Percy Adams. 6 plates, 7 illustrations. xlvii + 376pp. 6½ x 9¼.
21900-3 Paperbound $3.00

INTERNATIONAL AIRLINE PHRASE BOOK IN SIX LANGUAGES, Joseph W. Bátor. Important phrases and sentences in English paralleled with French, German, Portuguese, Italian, Spanish equivalents, covering all possible airport-travel situations; created for airline personnel as well as tourist by Language Chief, Pan American Airlines. xiv + 204pp.
22017-6 Paperbound $2.00

STAGE COACH AND TAVERN DAYS, Alice Morse Earle. Detailed, lively account of the early days of taverns; their uses and importance in the social, political and military life; furnishings and decorations; locations; food and drink; tavern signs, etc. Second half covers every aspect of early travel; the roads, coaches, drivers, etc. Nostalgic, charming, packed with fascinating material. 157 illustrations, mostly photographs. xiv + 449pp.
22518-6 Paperbound $4.00

NORSE DISCOVERIES AND EXPLORATIONS IN NORTH AMERICA, Hjalmar R. Holand. The perplexing Kensington Stone, found in Minnesota at the end of the 19th century. Is it a record of a Scandinavian expedition to North America in the 14th century? Or is it one of the most successful hoaxes in history? A scientific detective investigation. Formerly *Westward from Vinland.* 31 photographs, 17 figures. x + 354pp.
22014-1 Paperbound $2.75

A BOOK OF OLD MAPS, compiled and edited by Emerson D. Fite and Archibald Freeman. 74 old maps offer an unusual survey of the discovery, settlement and growth of America down to the close of the Revolutionary war: maps showing Norse settlements in Greenland, the explorations of Columbus, Verrazano, Cabot, Champlain, Joliet, Drake, Hudson, etc., campaigns of Revolutionary war battles, and much more. Each map is accompanied by a brief historical essay. xvi + 299pp. 11 x 13¾.
22084-2 Paperbound $6.00

POEMS OF ANNE BRADSTREET, edited with an introduction by Robert Hutchinson. A new selection of poems by America's first poet and perhaps the first significant woman poet in the English language. 48 poems display her development in works of considerable variety—love poems, domestic poems, religious meditations, formal elegies, "quaternions," etc. Notes, bibliography. viii + 222pp.
22160-1 Paperbound $2.00

THREE GOTHIC NOVELS: THE CASTLE OF OTRANTO BY HORACE WALPOLE; VATHEK BY WILLIAM BECKFORD; THE VAMPYRE BY JOHN POLIDORI, WITH FRAGMENT OF A NOVEL BY LORD BYRON, edited by E. F. Bleiler. The first Gothic novel, by Walpole; the finest Oriental tale in English, by Beckford; powerful Romantic supernatural story in versions by Polidori and Byron. All extremely important in history of literature; all still exciting, packed with supernatural thrills, ghosts, haunted castles, magic, etc. xl + 291pp.
21232-7 Paperbound $2.50

THE BEST TALES OF HOFFMANN, E. T. A. Hoffmann. 10 of Hoffmann's most important stories, in modern re-editings of standard translations: Nutcracker and the King of Mice, Signor Formica, Automata, The Sandman, Rath Krespel, The Golden Flowerpot, Master Martin the Cooper, The Mines of Falun, The King's Betrothed, A New Year's Eve Adventure. 7 illustrations by Hoffmann. Edited by E. F. Bleiler. xxxix + 419pp.
21793-0 Paperbound $3.00

GHOST AND HORROR STORIES OF AMBROSE BIERCE, Ambrose Bierce. 23 strikingly modern stories of the horrors latent in the human mind: The Eyes of the Panther, The Damned Thing, An Occurrence at Owl Creek Bridge, An Inhabitant of Carcosa, etc., plus the dream-essay, Visions of the Night. Edited by E. F. Bleiler. xxii + 199pp.
20767-6 Paperbound $1.50

BEST GHOST STORIES OF J. S. LeFANU, J. Sheridan LeFanu. Finest stories by Victorian master often considered greatest supernatural writer of all. Carmilla, Green Tea, The Haunted Baronet, The Familiar, and 12 others. Most never before available in the U. S. A. Edited by E. F. Bleiler. 8 illustrations from Victorian publications. xvii + 467pp.
20415-4 Paperbound $3.00

MATHEMATICAL FOUNDATIONS OF INFORMATION THEORY, A. I. Khinchin. Comprehensive introduction to work of Shannon, McMillan, Feinstein and Khinchin, placing these investigations on a rigorous mathematical basis. Covers entropy concept in probability theory, uniqueness theorem, Shannon's inequality, ergodic sources, the E property, martingale concept, noise, Feinstein's fundamental lemma, Shanon's first and second theorems. Translated by R. A. Silverman and M. D. Friedman. iii + 120pp.
60434-9 Paperbound $1.75

SEVEN SCIENCE FICTION NOVELS, H. G. Wells. The standard collection of the great novels. Complete, unabridged. *First Men in the Moon, Island of Dr. Moreau, War of the Worlds, Food of the Gods, Invisible Man, Time Machine, In the Days of the Comet.* Not only science fiction fans, but every educated person owes it to himself to read these novels. 1015pp.
20264-X Clothbound $5.00

JIM WHITEWOLF: THE LIFE OF A KIOWA APACHE INDIAN, Charles S. Brant, editor. Spans transition between native life and acculturation period, 1880 on. Kiowa culture, personal life pattern, religion and the supernatural, the Ghost Dance, breakdown in the White Man's world, similar material. 1 map. xii + 144pp.
22015-X Paperbound $1.75

THE NATIVE TRIBES OF CENTRAL AUSTRALIA, Baldwin Spencer and F. J. Gillen. Basic book in anthropology, devoted to full coverage of the Arunta and Warramunga tribes; the source for knowledge about kinship systems, material and social culture, religion, etc. Still unsurpassed. 121 photographs, 89 drawings. xviii + 669pp.
21775-2 Paperbound $5.00

MALAY MAGIC, Walter W. Skeat. Classic (1900); still the definitive work on the folklore and popular religion of the Malay peninsula. Describes marriage rites, birth spirits and ceremonies, medicine, dances, games, war and weapons, etc. Extensive quotes from original sources, many magic charms translated into English. 35 illustrations. Preface by Charles Otto Blagden. xxiv + 685pp.
21760-4 Paperbound $4.00

HEAVENS ON EARTH: UTOPIAN COMMUNITIES IN AMERICA, 1680-1880, Mark Holloway. The finest nontechnical account of American utopias, from the early Woman in the Wilderness, Ephrata, Rappites to the enormous mid 19th-century efflorescence; Shakers, New Harmony, Equity Stores, Fourier's Phalanxes, Oneida, Amana, Fruitlands, etc. "Entertaining and very instructive." *Times Literary Supplement*. 15 illustrations. 246pp.
21593-8 Paperbound $2.00

LONDON LABOUR AND THE LONDON POOR, Henry Mayhew. Earliest (c. 1850) sociological study in English, describing myriad subcultures of London poor. Particularly remarkable for the thousands of pages of direct testimony taken from the lips of London prostitutes, thieves, beggars, street sellers, chimney-sweepers, street-musicians, "mudlarks," "pure-finders," rag-gatherers, "running-patterers," dock laborers, cab-men, and hundreds of others, quoted directly in this massive work. An extraordinarily vital picture of London emerges. 110 illustrations. Total of lxxvi + 1951pp. 6⅝ x 10.
21934-8, 21935-6, 21936-4, 21937-2 Four volumes, Paperbound $14.00

HISTORY OF THE LATER ROMAN EMPIRE, J. B. Bury. Eloquent, detailed reconstruction of Western and Byzantine Roman Empire by a major historian, from the death of Theodosius I (395 A.D.) to the death of Justinian (565). Extensive quotations from contemporary sources; full coverage of important Roman and foreign figures of the time. xxxiv + 965pp. 21829-5 Record, book, album. Monaural. $3.50

AN INTELLECTUAL AND CULTURAL HISTORY OF THE WESTERN WORLD, Harry Elmer Barnes. Monumental study, tracing the development of the accomplishments that make up human culture. Every aspect of man's achievement surveyed from its origins in the Paleolithic to the present day (1964); social structures, ideas, economic systems, art, literature, technology, mathematics, the sciences, medicine, religion, jurisprudence, etc. Evaluations of the contributions of scores of great men. 1964 edition, revised and edited by scholars in the many fields represented. Total of xxix + 1381pp. 21275-0, 21276-9, 21277-7 Three volumes, Paperbound $7.75

THE RED FAIRY BOOK, Andrew Lang. Lang's color fairy books have long been children's favorites. This volume includes Rapunzel, Jack and the Bean-stalk and 35 other stories, familiar and unfamiliar. 4 plates, 93 illustrations x + 367pp.
21673-X Paperbound $2.50

THE BLUE FAIRY BOOK, Andrew Lang. Lang's tales come from all countries and all times. Here are 37 tales from Grimm, the Arabian Nights, Greek Mythology, and other fascinating sources. 8 plates, 130 illustrations. xi + 390pp.
21437-0 Paperbound $2.50

HOUSEHOLD STORIES BY THE BROTHERS GRIMM. Classic English-language edition of the well-known tales — Rumpelstiltskin, Snow White, Hansel and Gretel, The Twelve Brothers, Faithful John, Rapunzel, Tom Thumb (52 stories in all). Translated into simple, straightforward English by Lucy Crane. Ornamented with headpieces, vignettes, elaborate decorative initials and a dozen full-page illustrations by Walter Crane. x + 269pp.
21080-4 Paperbound $2.50

THE MERRY ADVENTURES OF ROBIN HOOD, Howard Pyle. The finest modern versions of the traditional ballads and tales about the great English outlaw. Howard Pyle's complete prose version, with every word, every illustration of the first edition. Do not confuse this facsimile of the original (1883) with modern editions that change text or illustrations. 23 plates plus many page decorations. xxii + 296pp.
22043-5 Paperbound $2.50

THE STORY OF KING ARTHUR AND HIS KNIGHTS, Howard Pyle. The finest children's version of the life of King Arthur; brilliantly retold by Pyle, with 48 of his most imaginative illustrations. xviii + 313pp. 6⅛ x 9¼.
21445-1 Paperbound $2.50

THE WONDERFUL WIZARD OF OZ, L. Frank Baum. America's finest children's book in facsimile of first edition with all Denslow illustrations in full color. The edition a child should have. Introduction by Martin Gardner. 23 color plates, scores of drawings. iv + 267pp.
20691-2 Paperbound $2.50

THE MARVELOUS LAND OF OZ, L. Frank Baum. The second Oz book, every bit as imaginative as the Wizard. The hero is a boy named Tip, but the Scarecrow and the Tin Woodman are back, as is the Oz magic. 16 color plates, 120 drawings by John R. Neill. 287pp.
20692-0 Paperbound $2.50

THE MAGICAL MONARCH OF MO, L. Frank Baum. Remarkable adventures in a land even stranger than Oz. The best of Baum's books not in the Oz series. 15 color plates and dozens of drawings by Frank Verbeck. xviii + 237pp.
21892-9 Paperbound $2.25

THE BAD CHILD'S BOOK OF BEASTS, MORE BEASTS FOR WORSE CHILDREN, A MORAL ALPHABET, Hilaire Belloc. Three complete humor classics in one volume. Be kind to the frog, and do not call him names . . . and 28 other whimsical animals. Familiar favorites and some not so well known. Illustrated by Basil Blackwell. 156pp.
(USO) 20749-8 Paperbound $1.50

EAST O' THE SUN AND WEST O' THE MOON, George W. Dasent. Considered the best of all translations of these Norwegian folk tales, this collection has been enjoyed by generations of children (and folklorists too). Includes True and Untrue, Why the Sea is Salt, East O' the Sun and West O' the Moon, Why the Bear is Stumpy-Tailed, Boots and the Troll, The Cock and the Hen, Rich Peter the Pedlar, and 52 more. The only edition with all 59 tales. 77 illustrations by Erik Werenskiold and Theodor Kittelsen. xv + 418pp. 22521-6 Paperbound $3.50

GOOPS AND HOW TO BE THEM, Gelett Burgess. Classic of tongue-in-cheek humor, masquerading as etiquette book. 87 verses, twice as many cartoons, show mischievous Goops as they demonstrate to children virtues of table manners, neatness, courtesy, etc. Favorite for generations. viii + 88pp. 6½ x 9¼. 22233-0 Paperbound $1.25

ALICE'S ADVENTURES UNDER GROUND, Lewis Carroll. The first version, quite different from the final *Alice in Wonderland,* printed out by Carroll himself with his own illustrations. Complete facsimile of the "million dollar" manuscript Carroll gave to Alice Liddell in 1864. Introduction by Martin Gardner. viii + 96pp. Title and dedication pages in color. 21482-6 Paperbound $1.25

THE BROWNIES, THEIR BOOK, Palmer Cox. Small as mice, cunning as foxes, exuberant and full of mischief, the Brownies go to the zoo, toy shop, seashore, circus, etc., in 24 verse adventures and 266 illustrations. Long a favorite, since their first appearance in St. Nicholas Magazine. xi + 144pp. 6⅝ x 9¼. 21265-3 Paperbound $1.75

SONGS OF CHILDHOOD, Walter De La Mare. Published (under the pseudonym Walter Ramal) when De La Mare was only 29, this charming collection has long been a favorite children's book. A facsimile of the first edition in paper, the 47 poems capture the simplicity of the nursery rhyme and the ballad, including such lyrics as I Met Eve, Tartary, The Silver Penny. vii + 106pp. 21972-0 Paperbound $1.25

THE COMPLETE NONSENSE OF EDWARD LEAR, Edward Lear. The finest 19th-century humorist-cartoonist in full: all nonsense limericks, zany alphabets, Owl and Pussycat, songs, nonsense botany, and more than 500 illustrations by Lear himself. Edited by Holbrook Jackson. xxix + 287pp. (USO) 20167-8 Paperbound $2.00

BILLY WHISKERS: THE AUTOBIOGRAPHY OF A GOAT, Frances Trego Montgomery. A favorite of children since the early 20th century, here are the escapades of that rambunctious, irresistible and mischievous goat—Billy Whiskers. Much in the spirit of *Peck's Bad Boy,* this is a book that children never tire of reading or hearing. All the original familiar illustrations by W. H. Fry are included: 6 color plates, 18 black and white drawings. 159pp. 22345-0 Paperbound $2.00

MOTHER GOOSE MELODIES. Faithful republication of the fabulously rare Munroe and Francis "copyright 1833" Boston edition—the most important Mother Goose collection, usually referred to as the "original." Familiar rhymes plus many rare ones, with wonderful old woodcut illustrations. Edited by E. F. Bleiler. 128pp. 4½ x 6⅜. 22577-1 Paperbound $1.25

AMERICAN FOOD AND GAME FISHES, David S. Jordan and Barton W. Evermann. Definitive source of information, detailed and accurate enough to enable the sportsman and nature lover to identify conclusively some 1,000 species and sub-species of North American fish, sought for food or sport. Coverage of range, physiology, habits, life history, food value. Best methods of capture, interest to the angler, advice on bait, fly-fishing, etc. 338 drawings and photographs. 1 + 574pp. 6⅝ x 9⅜.
22383-1 Paperbound $4.50

THE FROG BOOK, Mary C. Dickerson. Complete with extensive finding keys, over 300 photographs, and an introduction to the general biology of frogs and toads, this is the classic non-technical study of Northeastern and Central species. 58 species; 290 photographs and 16 color plates. xvii + 253pp.
21973-9 Paperbound $4.00

THE MOTH BOOK: A GUIDE TO THE MOTHS OF NORTH AMERICA, William J. Holland. Classical study, eagerly sought after and used for the past 60 years. Clear identification manual to more than 2,000 different moths, largest manual in existence. General information about moths, capturing, mounting, classifying, etc., followed by species by species descriptions. 263 illustrations plus 48 color plates show almost every species, full size. 1968 edition, preface, nomenclature changes by A. E. Brower. xxiv + 479pp. of text. 6½ x 9¼.
21948-8 Paperbound $5.00

THE SEA-BEACH AT EBB-TIDE, Augusta Foote Arnold. Interested amateur can identify hundreds of marine plants and animals on coasts of North America; marine algae; seaweeds; squids; hermit crabs; horse shoe crabs; shrimps; corals; sea anemones; etc. Species descriptions cover: structure; food; reproductive cycle; size; shape; color; habitat; etc. Over 600 drawings. 85 plates. xii + 490pp.
21949-6 Paperbound $3.50

COMMON BIRD SONGS, Donald J. Borror. 33⅓ 12-inch record presents songs of 60 important birds of the eastern United States. A thorough, serious record which provides several examples for each bird, showing different types of song, individual variations, etc. Inestimable identification aid for birdwatcher. 32-page booklet gives text about birds and songs, with illustration for each bird.
21829-5 Record, book, album. Monaural. $2.75

FADS AND FALLACIES IN THE NAME OF SCIENCE, Martin Gardner. Fair, witty appraisal of cranks and quacks of science: Atlantis, Lemuria, hollow earth, flat earth, Velikovsky, orgone energy, Dianetics, flying saucers, Bridey Murphy, food fads, medical fads, perpetual motion, etc. Formerly "In the Name of Science." x + 363pp.
20394-8 Paperbound $2.00

HOAXES, Curtis D. MacDougall. Exhaustive, unbelievably rich account of great hoaxes: Locke's moon hoax, Shakespearean forgeries, sea serpents, Loch Ness monster, Cardiff giant, John Wilkes Booth's mummy, Disumbrationist school of art, dozens more; also journalism, psychology of hoaxing. 54 illustrations. xi + 338pp.
20465-0 Paperbound $2.75

LAST AND FIRST MEN AND STAR MAKER, TWO SCIENCE FICTION NOVELS, Olaf Stapledon. Greatest future histories in science fiction. In the first, human intelligence is the "hero," through strange paths of evolution, interplanetary invasions, incredible technologies, near extinctions and reemergences. Star Maker describes the quest of a band of star rovers for intelligence itself, through time and space: weird inhuman civilizations, crustacean minds, symbiotic worlds, etc. Complete, unabridged. v + 438pp. 21962-3 Paperbound $2.50

THREE PROPHETIC NOVELS, H. G. WELLS. Stages of a consistently planned future for mankind. *When the Sleeper Wakes,* and *A Story of the Days to Come,* anticipate *Brave New World* and *1984,* in the 21st Century; *The Time Machine,* only complete version in print, shows farther future and the end of mankind. All show Wells's greatest gifts as storyteller and novelist. Edited by E. F. Bleiler. x + 335pp. (USO) 20605-X Paperbound $2.50

THE DEVIL'S DICTIONARY, Ambrose Bierce. America's own Oscar Wilde—Ambrose Bierce—offers his barbed iconoclastic wisdom in over 1,000 definitions hailed by H. L. Mencken as "some of the most gorgeous witticisms in the English language." 145pp. 20487-1 Paperbound $1.25

MAX AND MORITZ, Wilhelm Busch. Great children's classic, father of comic strip, of two bad boys, Max and Moritz. Also Ker and Plunk (Plisch und Plumm), Cat and Mouse, Deceitful Henry, Ice-Peter, The Boy and the Pipe, and five other pieces. Original German, with English translation. Edited by H. Arthur Klein; translations by various hands and H. Arthur Klein. vi + 216pp. 20181-3 Paperbound $2.00

PIGS IS PIGS AND OTHER FAVORITES, Ellis Parker Butler. The title story is one of the best humor short stories, as Mike Flannery obfuscates biology and English. Also included, That Pup of Murchison's, The Great American Pie Company, and Perkins of Portland. 14 illustrations. v + 109pp. 21532-6 Paperbound $1.25

THE PETERKIN PAPERS, Lucretia P. Hale. It takes genius to be as stupidly mad as the Peterkins, as they decide to become wise, celebrate the "Fourth," keep a cow, and otherwise strain the resources of the Lady from Philadelphia. Basic book of American humor. 153 illustrations. 219pp. 20794-3 Paperbound $1.50

PERRAULT'S FAIRY TALES, translated by A. E. Johnson and S. R. Littlewood, with 34 full-page illustrations by Gustave Doré. All the original Perrault stories—Cinderella, Sleeping Beauty, Bluebeard, Little Red Riding Hood, Puss in Boots, Tom Thumb, etc.—with their witty verse morals and the magnificent illustrations of Doré. One of the five or six great books of European fairy tales. viii + 117pp. 8⅛ x 11. 22311-6 Paperbound $2.00

OLD HUNGARIAN FAIRY TALES, Baroness Orczy. Favorites translated and adapted by author of the *Scarlet Pimpernel.* Eight fairy tales include "The Suitors of Princess Fire-Fly," "The Twin Hunchbacks," "Mr. Cuttlefish's Love Story," and "The Enchanted Cat." This little volume of magic and adventure will captivate children as it has for generations. 90 drawings by Montagu Barstow. 96pp. (USO) 22293-4 Paperbound $1.95

CATALOGUE OF DOVER BOOKS

ADVENTURES OF AN AFRICAN SLAVER, Theodore Canot. Edited by Brantz Mayer. A detailed portrayal of slavery and the slave trade, 1820-1840. Canot, an established trader along the African coast, describes the slave economy of the African kingdoms, the treatment of captured negroes, the extensive journeys in the interior to gather slaves, slave revolts and their suppression, harems, bribes, and much more. Full and unabridged republication of 1854 edition. Introduction by Malcom Cowley. 16 illustrations. xvii + 448pp. 22456-2 Paperbound $3.50

MY BONDAGE AND MY FREEDOM, Frederick Douglass. Born and brought up in slavery, Douglass witnessed its horrors and experienced its cruelties, but went on to become one of the most outspoken forces in the American anti-slavery movement. Considered the best of his autobiographies, this book graphically describes the inhuman treatment of slaves, its effects on slave owners and slave families, and how Douglass's determination led him to a new life. Unaltered reprint of 1st (1855) edition. xxxii + 464pp. 22457-0 Paperbound $2.50

THE INDIANS' BOOK, recorded and edited by Natalie Curtis. Lore, music, narratives, dozens of drawings by Indians themselves from an authoritative and important survey of native culture among Plains, Southwestern, Lake and Pueblo Indians. Standard work in popular ethnomusicology. 149 songs in full notation. 23 drawings, 23 photos. xxxi + 584pp. 6⅝ x 9⅜. 21939-9 Paperbound $4.50

DICTIONARY OF AMERICAN PORTRAITS, edited by Hayward and Blanche Cirker. 4024 portraits of 4000 most important Americans, colonial days to 1905 (with a few important categories, like Presidents, to present). Pioneers, explorers, colonial figures, U. S. officials, politicians, writers, military and naval men, scientists, inventors, manufacturers, jurists, actors, historians, educators, notorious figures, Indian chiefs, etc. All authentic contemporary likenesses. The only work of its kind in existence; supplements all biographical sources for libraries. Indispensable to anyone working with American history. 8,000-item classified index, finding lists, other aids. xiv + 756pp. 9¼ x 12¾. 21823-6 Clothbound $30.00

TRITTON'S GUIDE TO BETTER WINE AND BEER MAKING FOR BEGINNERS, S. M. Tritton. All you need to know to make family-sized quantities of over 100 types of grape, fruit, herb and vegetable wines; as well as beers, mead, cider, etc. Complete recipes, advice as to equipment, procedures such as fermenting, bottling, and storing wines. Recipes given in British, U. S., and metric measures. Accompanying booklet lists sources in U. S. A. where ingredients may be bought, and additional information. 11 illustrations. 157pp. 5⅝ x 8⅛. (USO) 22090-7 Clothbound $3.50

GARDENING WITH HERBS FOR FLAVOR AND FRAGRANCE, Helen M. Fox. How to grow herbs in your own garden, how to use them in your cooking (over 55 recipes included), legends and myths associated with each species, uses in medicine, perfumes, etc.—these are elements of one of the few books written especially for American herb fanciers. Guides you step-by-step from soil preparation to harvesting and storage for each type of herb. 12 drawings by Louise Mansfield. xiv + 334pp. 22540-2 Paperbound $2.50

THE PHILOSOPHY OF THE UPANISHADS, Paul Deussen. Clear, detailed statement of upanishadic system of thought, generally considered among best available. History of these works, full exposition of system emergent from them, parallel concepts in the West. Translated by A. S. Geden. xiv + 429pp.
21616-0 Paperbound $3.00

LANGUAGE, TRUTH AND LOGIC, Alfred J. Ayer. Famous, remarkably clear introduction to the Vienna and Cambridge schools of Logical Positivism; function of philosophy, elimination of metaphysical thought, nature of analysis, similar topics. "Wish I had written it myself," Bertrand Russell. 2nd, 1946 edition. 160pp.
20010-8 Paperbound $1.35

THE GUIDE FOR THE PERPLEXED, Moses Maimonides. Great classic of medieval Judaism, major attempt to reconcile revealed religion (Pentateuch, commentaries) and Aristotelian philosophy. Enormously important in all Western thought. Unabridged Friedländer translation. 50-page introduction. lix + 414pp.
(USO) 20351-4 Paperbound $2.50

OCCULT AND SUPERNATURAL PHENOMENA, D. H. Rawcliffe. Full, serious study of the most persistent delusions of mankind: crystal gazing, mediumistic trance, stigmata, lycanthropy, fire walking, dowsing, telepathy, ghosts, ESP, etc., and their relation to common forms of abnormal psychology. Formerly *Illusions and Delusions of the Supernatural and the Occult.* iii + 551pp.
20503-7 Paperbound $3.50

THE EGYPTIAN BOOK OF THE DEAD: THE PAPYRUS OF ANI, E. A. Wallis Budge. Full hieroglyphic text, interlinear transliteration of sounds, word for word translation, then smooth, connected translation; Theban recension. Basic work in Ancient Egyptian civilization; now even more significant than ever for historical importance, dilation of consciousness, etc. clvi + 377pp. 6½ x 9¼.
21866-X Paperbound $3.95

PSYCHOLOGY OF MUSIC, Carl E. Seashore. Basic, thorough survey of everything known about psychology of music up to 1940's; essential reading for psychologists, musicologists. Physical acoustics; auditory apparatus; relationship of physical sound to perceived sound; role of the mind in sorting, altering, suppressing, creating sound sensations; musical learning, testing for ability, absolute pitch, other topics. Records of Caruso, Menuhin analyzed. 88 figures. xix + 408pp.
21851-1 Paperbound $2.75

THE I CHING (THE BOOK OF CHANGES), translated by James Legge. Complete translated text plus appendices by Confucius, of perhaps the most penetrating divination book ever compiled. Indispensable to all study of early Oriental civilizations. 3 plates. xxiii + 448pp. 21062-6 Paperbound $3.00

THE UPANISHADS, translated by Max Müller. Twelve classical upanishads: Chandogya, Kena, Aitareya, Kaushitaki, Isa, Katha, Mundaka, Taittiriyaka, Brhadaranyaka, Svetasvatara, Prasna, Maitriyana. 160-page introduction, analysis by Prof. Müller. Total of 826pp. 20398-0, 20399-9 Two volumes, Paperbound $5.00

JOHANN SEBASTIAN BACH, Philipp Spitta. One of the great classics of musicology, this definitive analysis of Bach's music (and life) has never been surpassed. Lucid, nontechnical analyses of hundreds of pieces (30 pages devoted to St. Matthew Passion, 26 to B Minor Mass). Also includes major analysis of 18th-century music. 450 musical examples. 40-page musical supplement. Total of xx + 1799pp.
(EUK) 22278-0, 22279-9 Two volumes, Clothbound $15.00

MOZART AND HIS PIANO CONCERTOS, Cuthbert Girdlestone. The only full-length study of an important area of Mozart's creativity. Provides detailed analyses of all 23 concertos, traces inspirational sources. 417 musical examples. Second edition. 509pp. (USO) 21271-8 Paperbound $3.50

THE PERFECT WAGNERITE: A COMMENTARY ON THE NIBLUNG'S RING, George Bernard Shaw. Brilliant and still relevant criticism in remarkable essays on Wagner's Ring cycle, Shaw's ideas on political and social ideology behind the plots, role of Leitmotifs, vocal requisites, etc. Prefaces. xxi + 136pp.
21707-8 Paperbound $1.50

DON GIOVANNI, W. A. Mozart. Complete libretto, modern English translation; biographies of composer and librettist; accounts of early performances and critical reaction. Lavishly illustrated. All the material you need to understand and appreciate this great work. Dover Opera Guide and Libretto Series; translated and introduced by Ellen Bleiler. 92 illustrations. 209pp.
21134-7 Paperbound $1.50

HIGH FIDELITY SYSTEMS: A LAYMAN'S GUIDE, Roy F. Allison. All the basic information you need for setting up your own audio system: high fidelity and stereo record players, tape records, F.M. Connections, adjusting tone arm, cartridge, checking needle alignment, positioning speakers, phasing speakers, adjusting hums, trouble-shooting, maintenance, and similar topics. Enlarged 1965 edition. More than 50 charts, diagrams, photos. iv + 91pp. 21514-8 Paperbound $1.25

REPRODUCTION OF SOUND, Edgar Villchur. Thorough coverage for laymen of high fidelity systems, reproducing systems in general, needles, amplifiers, preamps, loudspeakers, feedback, explaining physical background. "A rare talent for making technicalities vividly comprehensible," R. Darrell, *High Fidelity*. 69 figures. iv + 92pp. 21515-6 Paperbound $1.00

HEAR ME TALKIN' TO YA: THE STORY OF JAZZ AS TOLD BY THE MEN WHO MADE IT, Nat Shapiro and Nat Hentoff. Louis Armstrong, Fats Waller, Jo Jones, Clarence Williams, Billy Holiday, Duke Ellington, Jelly Roll Morton and dozens of other jazz greats tell how it was in Chicago's South Side, New Orleans, depression Harlem and the modern West Coast as jazz was born and grew. xvi + 429pp.
21726-4 Paperbound $2.50

FABLES OF AESOP, translated by Sir Roger L'Estrange. A reproduction of the very rare 1931 Paris edition; a selection of the most interesting fables, together with 50 imaginative drawings by Alexander Calder. v + 128pp. 6½x9¼.
21780-9 Paperbound $1.25

How to Know the Wild Flowers, Mrs. William Starr Dana. This is the classical book of American wildflowers (of the Eastern and Central United States), used by hundreds of thousands. Covers over 500 species, arranged in extremely easy to use color and season groups. Full descriptions, much plant lore. This Dover edition is the fullest ever compiled, with tables of nomenclature changes. 174 full-page plates by M. Satterlee. xii + 418pp. 20332-8 Paperbound $2.75

Our Plant Friends and Foes, William Atherton DuPuy. History, economic importance, essential botanical information and peculiarities of 25 common forms of plant life are provided in this book in an entertaining and charming style. Covers food plants (potatoes, apples, beans, wheat, almonds, bananas, etc.), flowers (lily, tulip, etc.), trees (pine, oak, elm, etc.), weeds, poisonous mushrooms and vines, gourds, citrus fruits, cotton, the cactus family, and much more. 108 illustrations. xiv + 290pp. 22272-1 Paperbound $2.50

How to Know the Ferns, Frances T. Parsons. Classic survey of Eastern and Central ferns, arranged according to clear, simple identification key. Excellent introduction to greatly neglected nature area. 57 illustrations and 42 plates. xvi + 215pp. 20740-4 Paperbound $2.00

Manual of the Trees of North America, Charles S. Sargent. America's foremost dendrologist provides the definitive coverage of North American trees and tree-like shrubs. 717 species fully described and illustrated: exact distribution, down to township; full botanical description; economic importance; description of subspecies and races; habitat, growth data; similar material. Necessary to every serious student of tree-life. Nomenclature revised to present. Over 100 locating keys. 783 illustrations. lii + 934pp. 20277-1, 20278-X Two volumes, Paperbound $6.00

Our Northern Shrubs, Harriet L. Keeler. Fine non-technical reference work identifying more than 225 important shrubs of Eastern and Central United States and Canada. Full text covering botanical description, habitat, plant lore, is paralleled with 205 full-page photographs of flowering or fruiting plants. Nomenclature revised by Edward G. Voss. One of few works concerned with shrubs. 205 plates, 35 drawings. xxviii + 521pp. 21989-5 Paperbound $3.75

The Mushroom Handbook, Louis C. C. Krieger. Still the best popular handbook: full descriptions of 259 species, cross references to another 200. Extremely thorough text enables you to identify, know all about any mushroom you are likely to meet in eastern and central U. S. A.: habitat, luminescence, poisonous qualities, use, folklore, etc. 32 color plates show over 50 mushrooms, also 126 other illustrations. Finding keys. vii + 560pp. 21861-9 Paperbound $3.95

Handbook of Birds of Eastern North America, Frank M. Chapman. Still much the best single-volume guide to the birds of Eastern and Central United States. Very full coverage of 675 species, with descriptions, life habits, distribution, similar data. All descriptions keyed to two-page color chart. With this single volume the average birdwatcher needs no other books. 1931 revised edition. 195 illustrations. xxxvi + 581pp. 21489-3 Paperbound $4.50

ALPHABETS AND ORNAMENTS, Ernst Lehner. Well-known pictorial source for decorative alphabets, script examples, cartouches, frames, decorative title pages, calligraphic initials, borders, similar material. 14th to 19th century, mostly European. Useful in almost any graphic arts designing, varied styles. 750 illustrations. 256pp. 7 x 10. 21905-4 Paperbound $4.00

PAINTING: A CREATIVE APPROACH, Norman Colquhoun. For the beginner simple guide provides an instructive approach to painting: major stumbling blocks for beginner; overcoming them, technical points; paints and pigments; oil painting; watercolor and other media and color. New section on "plastic" paints. Glossary. Formerly *Paint Your Own Pictures.* 221pp. 22000-1 Paperbound $1.75

THE ENJOYMENT AND USE OF COLOR, Walter Sargent. Explanation of the relations between colors themselves and between colors in nature and art, including hundreds of little-known facts about color values, intensities, effects of high and low illumination, complementary colors. Many practical hints for painters, references to great masters. 7 color plates, 29 illustrations. x + 274pp. 20944-X Paperbound $2.75

THE NOTEBOOKS OF LEONARDO DA VINCI, compiled and edited by Jean Paul Richter. 1566 extracts from original manuscripts reveal the full range of Leonardo's versatile genius: all his writings on painting, sculpture, architecture, anatomy, astronomy, geography, topography, physiology, mining, music, etc., in both Italian and English, with 186 plates of manuscript pages and more than 500 additional drawings. Includes studies for the Last Supper, the lost Sforza monument, and other works. Total of xlvii + 866pp. 7⅞ x 10¾. 22572-0, 22573-9 Two volumes, Paperbound $10.00

MONTGOMERY WARD CATALOGUE OF 1895. Tea gowns, yards of flannel and pillow-case lace, stereoscopes, books of gospel hymns, the New Improved Singer Sewing Machine, side saddles, milk skimmers, straight-edged razors, high-button shoes, spittoons, and on and on . . . listing some 25,000 items, practically all illustrated. Essential to the shoppers of the 1890's, it is our truest record of the spirit of the period. Unaltered reprint of Issue No. 57, Spring and Summer 1895. Introduction by Boris Emmet. Innumerable illustrations. xiii + 624pp. 8½ x 11⅝. 22377-9 Paperbound $6.95

THE CRYSTAL PALACE EXHIBITION ILLUSTRATED CATALOGUE (LONDON, 1851). One of the wonders of the modern world—the Crystal Palace Exhibition in which all the nations of the civilized world exhibited their achievements in the arts and sciences—presented in an equally important illustrated catalogue. More than 1700 items pictured with accompanying text—ceramics, textiles, cast-iron work, carpets, pianos, sleds, razors, wall-papers, billiard tables, beehives, silverware and hundreds of other artifacts—represent the focal point of Victorian culture in the Western World. Probably the largest collection of Victorian decorative art ever assembled—indispensable for antiquarians and designers. Unabridged republication of the Art-Journal Catalogue of the Great Exhibition of 1851, with all terminal essays. New introduction by John Gloag, F.S.A. xxxiv + 426pp. 9 x 12. 22503-8 Paperbound $4.50

VISUAL ILLUSIONS: THEIR CAUSES, CHARACTERISTICS, AND APPLICATIONS, Matthew Luckiesh. Thorough description and discussion of optical illusion, geometric and perspective, particularly; size and shape distortions, illusions of color, of motion; natural illusions; use of illusion in art and magic, industry, etc. Most useful today with op art, also for classical art. Scores of effects illustrated. Introduction by William H. Ittleson. 100 illustrations. xxi + 252pp.
21530-X Paperbound $2.00

A HANDBOOK OF ANATOMY FOR ART STUDENTS, Arthur Thomson. Thorough, virtually exhaustive coverage of skeletal structure, musculature, etc. Full text, supplemented by anatomical diagrams and drawings and by photographs of undraped figures. Unique in its comparison of male and female forms, pointing out differences of contour, texture, form. 211 figures, 40 drawings, 86 photographs. xx + 459pp. 5⅜ x 8⅜.
21163-0 Paperbound $3.50

150 MASTERPIECES OF DRAWING, Selected by Anthony Toney. Full page reproductions of drawings from the early 16th to the end of the 18th century, all beautifully reproduced: Rembrandt, Michelangelo, Dürer, Fragonard, Urs, Graf, Wouwerman, many others. First-rate browsing book, model book for artists. xviii + 150pp. 8⅜ x 11¼.
21032-4 Paperbound $2.50

THE LATER WORK OF AUBREY BEARDSLEY, Aubrey Beardsley. Exotic, erotic, ironic masterpieces in full maturity: Comedy Ballet, Venus and Tannhauser, Pierrot, Lysistrata, Rape of the Lock, Savoy material, Ali Baba, Volpone, etc. This material revolutionized the art world, and is still powerful, fresh, brilliant. With *The Early Work*, all Beardsley's finest work. 174 plates, 2 in color. xiv + 176pp. 8⅛ x 11.
21817-1 Paperbound $3.00

DRAWINGS OF REMBRANDT, Rembrandt van Rijn. Complete reproduction of fabulously rare edition by Lippmann and Hofstede de Groot, completely reedited, updated, improved by Prof. Seymour Slive, Fogg Museum. Portraits, Biblical sketches, landscapes, Oriental types, nudes, episodes from classical mythology—All Rembrandt's fertile genius. Also selection of drawings by his pupils and followers. "Stunning volumes," *Saturday Review.* 550 illustrations. lxxviii + 552pp. 9⅛ x 12¼.
21485-0, 21486-9 Two volumes, Paperbound $10.00

THE DISASTERS OF WAR, Francisco Goya. One of the masterpieces of Western civilization—83 etchings that record Goya's shattering, bitter reaction to the Napoleonic war that swept through Spain after the insurrection of 1808 and to war in general. Reprint of the first edition, with three additional plates from Boston's Museum of Fine Arts. All plates facsimile size. Introduction by Philip Hofer, Fogg Museum. v + 97pp. 9⅜ x 8¼.
21872-4 Paperbound $2.00

GRAPHIC WORKS OF ODILON REDON. Largest collection of Redon's graphic works ever assembled: 172 lithographs, 28 etchings and engravings, 9 drawings. These include some of his most famous works. All the plates from *Odilon Redon: oeuvre graphique complet,* plus additional plates. New introduction and caption translations by Alfred Werner. 209 illustrations. xxvii + 209pp. 9⅛ x 12¼.
21966-8 Paperbound $4.00

TWO LITTLE SAVAGES; BEING THE ADVENTURES OF TWO BOYS WHO LIVED AS INDIANS AND WHAT THEY LEARNED, Ernest Thompson Seton. Great classic of nature and boyhood provides a vast range of woodlore in most palatable form, a genuinely entertaining story. Two farm boys build a teepee in woods and live in it for a month, working out Indian solutions to living problems, star lore, birds and animals, plants, etc. 293 illustrations. vii + 286pp.

20985-7 Paperbound $2.50

PETER PIPER'S PRACTICAL PRINCIPLES OF PLAIN & PERFECT PRONUNCIATION. Alliterative jingles and tongue-twisters of surprising charm, that made their first appearance in America about 1830. Republished in full with the spirited woodcut illustrations from this earliest American edition. 32pp. 4½ x 6⅜.

22560-7 Paperbound $1.00

SCIENCE EXPERIMENTS AND AMUSEMENTS FOR CHILDREN, Charles Vivian. 73 easy experiments, requiring only materials found at home or easily available, such as candles, coins, steel wool, etc.; illustrate basic phenomena like vacuum, simple chemical reaction, etc. All safe. Modern, well-planned. Formerly *Science Games for Children*. 102 photos, numerous drawings. 96pp. 6⅛ x 9¼.

21856-2 Paperbound $1.25

AN INTRODUCTION TO CHESS MOVES AND TACTICS SIMPLY EXPLAINED, Leonard Barden. Informal intermediate introduction, quite strong in explaining reasons for moves. Covers basic material, tactics, important openings, traps, positional play in middle game, end game. Attempts to isolate patterns and recurrent configurations. Formerly *Chess*. 58 figures. 102pp. (USO) 21210-6 Paperbound $1.25

LASKER'S MANUAL OF CHESS, Dr. Emanuel Lasker. Lasker was not only one of the five great World Champions, he was also one of the ablest expositors, theorists, and analysts. In many ways, his Manual, permeated with his philosophy of battle, filled with keen insights, is one of the greatest works ever written on chess. Filled with analyzed games by the great players. A single-volume library that will profit almost any chess player, beginner or master. 308 diagrams. xli x 349pp.

20640-8 Paperbound $2.75

THE MASTER BOOK OF MATHEMATICAL RECREATIONS, Fred Schuh. In opinion of many the finest work ever prepared on mathematical puzzles, stunts, recreations; exhaustively thorough explanations of mathematics involved, analysis of effects, citation of puzzles and games. Mathematics involved is elementary. Translated by F. Göbel. 194 figures. xxiv + 430pp. 22134-2 Paperbound $3.00

MATHEMATICS, MAGIC AND MYSTERY, Martin Gardner. Puzzle editor for Scientific American explains mathematics behind various mystifying tricks: card tricks, stage "mind reading," coin and match tricks, counting out games, geometric dissections, etc. Probability sets, theory of numbers clearly explained. Also provides more than 400 tricks, guaranteed to work, that you can do. 135 illustrations. xii + 176pp.

20338-2 Paperbound $1.50

THE ARCHITECTURE OF COUNTRY HOUSES, Andrew J. Downing. Together with Vaux's *Villas and Cottages* this is the basic book for Hudson River Gothic architecture of the middle Victorian period. Full, sound discussions of general aspects of housing, architecture, style, decoration, furnishing, together with scores of detailed house plans, illustrations of specific buildings, accompanied by full text. Perhaps the most influential single American architectural book. 1850 edition. Introduction by J. Stewart Johnson. 321 figures, 34 architectural designs. xvi + 560pp.

22003-6 Paperbound $4.00

LOST EXAMPLES OF COLONIAL ARCHITECTURE, John Mead Howells. Full-page photographs of buildings that have disappeared or been so altered as to be denatured, including many designed by major early American architects. 245 plates. xvii + 248pp. 7⅞ x 10¾. 21143-6 Paperbound $3.50

DOMESTIC ARCHITECTURE OF THE AMERICAN COLONIES AND OF THE EARLY REPUBLIC, Fiske Kimball. Foremost architect and restorer of Williamsburg and Monticello covers nearly 200 homes between 1620-1825. Architectural details, construction, style features, special fixtures, floor plans, etc. Generally considered finest work in its area. 219 illustrations of houses, doorways, windows, capital mantels. xx + 314pp. 7⅞ x 10¾. 21743-4 Paperbound $4.00

EARLY AMERICAN ROOMS: 1650-1858, edited by Russell Hawes Kettell. Tour of 12 rooms, each representative of a different era in American history and each furnished, decorated, designed and occupied in the style of the era. 72 plans and elevations, 8-page color section, etc., show fabrics, wall papers, arrangements, etc. Full descriptive text. xvii + 200pp. of text. 8⅜ x 11¼.

21633-0 Paperbound $5.00

THE FITZWILLIAM VIRGINAL BOOK, edited by J. Fuller Maitland and W. B. Squire. Full modern printing of famous early 17th-century ms. volume of 300 works by Morley, Byrd, Bull, Gibbons, etc. For piano or other modern keyboard instrument; easy to read format. xxxvi + 938pp. 8⅜ x 11.

21068-5, 21069-3 Two volumes, Paperbound$10.00

KEYBOARD MUSIC, Johann Sebastian Bach. Bach Gesellschaft edition. A rich selection of Bach's masterpieces for the harpsichord: the six English Suites, six French Suites, the six Partitas (Clavierübung part I), the Goldberg Variations (Clavierübung part IV), the fifteen Two-Part Inventions and the fifteen Three-Part Sinfonias. Clearly reproduced on large sheets with ample margins; eminently playable. vi + 312pp. 8⅛ x 11. 22360-4 Paperbound $5.00

THE MUSIC OF BACH: AN INTRODUCTION, Charles Sanford Terry. A fine, nontechnical introduction to Bach's music, both instrumental and vocal. Covers organ music, chamber music, passion music, other types. Analyzes themes, developments, innovations. x + 114pp. 21075-8 Paperbound $1.25

BEETHOVEN AND HIS NINE SYMPHONIES, Sir George Grove. Noted British musicologist provides best history, analysis, commentary on symphonies. Very thorough, rigorously accurate; necessary to both advanced student and amateur music lover. 436 musical passages. vii + 407 pp. 20334-4 Paperbound $2.75

DESIGN BY ACCIDENT; A BOOK OF "ACCIDENTAL EFFECTS" FOR ARTISTS AND DESIGNERS, James F. O'Brien. Create your own unique, striking, imaginative effects by "controlled accident" interaction of materials: paints and lacquers, oil and water based paints, splatter, crackling materials, shatter, similar items. Everything you do will be different; first book on this limitless art, so useful to both fine artist and commercial artist. Full instructions. 192 plates showing "accidents," 8 in color. viii + 215pp. 8⅜ x 11¼.   21942-9 Paperbound $3.50

THE BOOK OF SIGNS, Rudolf Koch. Famed German type designer draws 493 beautiful symbols: religious, mystical, alchemical, imperial, property marks, runes, etc. Remarkable fusion of traditional and modern. Good for suggestions of timelessness, smartness, modernity. Text. vi + 104pp. 6⅛ x 9¼.
                                        20162-7 Paperbound $1.25

HISTORY OF INDIAN AND INDONESIAN ART, Ananda K. Coomaraswamy. An unabridged republication of one of the finest books by a great scholar in Eastern art. Rich in descriptive material, history, social backgrounds; Sunga reliefs, Rajput paintings, Gupta temples, Burmese frescoes, textiles, jewelry, sculpture, etc. 400 photos. viii + 423pp. 6⅜ x 9¾.   21436-2 Paperbound $4.00

PRIMITIVE ART, Franz Boas. America's foremost anthropologist surveys textiles, ceramics, woodcarving, basketry, metalwork, etc.; patterns, technology, creation of symbols, style origins. All areas of world, but very full on Northwest Coast Indians. More than 350 illustrations of baskets, boxes, totem poles, weapons, etc. 378 pp.
                                        20025-6 Paperbound $3.00

THE GENTLEMAN AND CABINET MAKER'S DIRECTOR, Thomas Chippendale. Full reprint (third edition, 1762) of most influential furniture book of all time, by master cabinetmaker. 200 plates, illustrating chairs, sofas, mirrors, tables, cabinets, plus 24 photographs of surviving pieces. Biographical introduction by N. Bienenstock. vi + 249pp. 9⅞ x 12¾.   21601-2 Paperbound $4.00

AMERICAN ANTIQUE FURNITURE, Edgar G. Miller, Jr. The basic coverage of all American furniture before 1840. Individual chapters cover type of furniture—clocks, tables, sideboards, etc.—chronologically, with inexhaustible wealth of data. More than 2100 photographs, all identified, commented on. Essential to all early American collectors. Introduction by H. E. Keyes. vi + 1106pp. 7⅞ x 10¾.
                    21599-7, 21600-4 Two volumes, Paperbound $11.00

PENNSYLVANIA DUTCH AMERICAN FOLK ART, Henry J. Kauffman. 279 photos, 28 drawings of tulipware, Fraktur script, painted tinware, toys, flowered furniture, quilts, samplers, hex signs, house interiors, etc. Full descriptive text. Excellent for tourist, rewarding for designer, collector. Map. 146pp. 7⅞ x 10¾.
                                        21205-X Paperbound $2.50

EARLY NEW ENGLAND GRAVESTONE RUBBINGS, Edmund V. Gillon, Jr. 43 photographs, 226 carefully reproduced rubbings show heavily symbolic, sometimes macabre early gravestones, up to early 19th century. Remarkable early American primitive art, occasionally strikingly beautiful; always powerful. Text. xxvi + 207pp. 8⅜ x 11¼.   21380-3 Paperbound $3.50

A HISTORY OF COSTUME, Carl Köhler. Definitive history, based on surviving pieces of clothing primarily, and paintings, statues, etc. secondarily. Highly readable text, supplemented by 594 illustrations of costumes of the ancient Mediterranean peoples, Greece and Rome, the Teutonic prehistoric period; costumes of the Middle Ages, Renaissance, Baroque, 18th and 19th centuries. Clear, measured patterns are provided for many clothing articles. Approach is practical throughout. Enlarged by Emma von Sichart. 464pp. 21030-8 Paperbound $3.50

ORIENTAL RUGS, ANTIQUE AND MODERN, Walter A. Hawley. A complete and authoritative treatise on the Oriental rug—where they are made, by whom and how, designs and symbols, characteristics in detail of the six major groups, how to distinguish them and how to buy them. Detailed technical data is provided on periods, weaves, warps, wefts, textures, sides, ends and knots, although no technical background is required for an understanding. 11 color plates, 80 halftones, 4 maps. vi + 320pp. 6⅛ x 9⅛. 22366-3 Paperbound $5.00

TEN BOOKS ON ARCHITECTURE, Vitruvius. By any standards the most important book on architecture ever written. Early Roman discussion of aesthetics of building, construction methods, orders, sites, and every other aspect of architecture has inspired, instructed architecture for about 2,000 years. Stands behind Palladio, Michelangelo, Bramante, Wren, countless others. Definitive Morris H. Morgan translation. 68 illustrations. xii + 331pp. 20645-9 Paperbound $3.50

THE FOUR BOOKS OF ARCHITECTURE, Andrea Palladio. Translated into every major Western European language in the two centuries following its publication in 1570, this has been one of the most influential books in the history of architecture. Complete reprint of the 1738 Isaac Ware edition. New introduction by Adolf Placzek, Columbia Univ. 216 plates. xxii + 110pp. of text. 9½ x 12¾. 21308-0 Clothbound $10.00

STICKS AND STONES: A STUDY OF AMERICAN ARCHITECTURE AND CIVILIZATION, Lewis Mumford. One of the great classics of American cultural history. American architecture from the medieval-inspired earliest forms to the early 20th century; evolution of structure and style, and reciprocal influences on environment. 21 photographic illustrations. 238pp. 20202-X Paperbound $2.00

THE AMERICAN BUILDER'S COMPANION, Asher Benjamin. The most widely used early 19th century architectural style and source book, for colonial up into Greek Revival periods. Extensive development of geometry of carpentering, construction of sashes, frames, doors, stairs; plans and elevations of domestic and other buildings. Hundreds of thousands of houses were built according to this book, now invaluable to historians, architects, restorers, etc. 1827 edition. 59 plates. 114pp. 7⅞ x 10¾. 22236-5 Paperbound $3.50

DUTCH HOUSES IN THE HUDSON VALLEY BEFORE 1776, Helen Wilkinson Reynolds. The standard survey of the Dutch colonial house and outbuildings, with constructional features, decoration, and local history associated with individual homesteads. Introduction by Franklin D. Roosevelt. Map. 150 illustrations. 469pp. 6⅝ x 9¼. 21469-9 Paperbound $4.00

AGAINST THE GRAIN (A REBOURS), Joris K. Huysmans. Filled with weird images, evidences of a bizarre imagination, exotic experiments with hallucinatory drugs, rich tastes and smells and the diversions of its sybarite hero Duc Jean des Esseintes, this classic novel pushed 19th-century literary decadence to its limits. Full unabridged edition. Do not confuse this with abridged editions generally sold. Introduction by Havelock Ellis. xlix + 206pp.   22190-3 Paperbound $2.00

VARIORUM SHAKESPEARE: HAMLET. Edited by Horace H. Furness; a landmark of American scholarship. Exhaustive footnotes and appendices treat all doubtful words and phrases, as well as suggested critical emendations throughout the play's history. First volume contains editor's own text, collated with all Quartos and Folios. Second volume contains full first Quarto, translations of Shakespeare's sources (Belleforest, and Saxo Grammaticus), Der Bestrafte Brudermord, and many essays on critical and historical points of interest by major authorities of past and present. Includes details of staging and costuming over the years. By far the best edition available for serious students of Shakespeare. Total of xx + 905pp.
21004-9, 21005-7, 2 volumes, Paperbound $7.00

A LIFE OF WILLIAM SHAKESPEARE, Sir Sidney Lee. This is the standard life of Shakespeare, summarizing everything known about Shakespeare and his plays. Incredibly rich in material, broad in coverage, clear and judicious, it has served thousands as the best introduction to Shakespeare. 1931 edition. 9 plates. xxix + 792pp.   (USO) 21967-4 Paperbound $3.75

MASTERS OF THE DRAMA, John Gassner. Most comprehensive history of the drama in print, covering every tradition from Greeks to modern Europe and America, including India, Far East, etc. Covers more than 800 dramatists, 2000 plays, with biographical material, plot summaries, theatre history, criticism, etc. "Best of its kind in English," New Republic. 77 illustrations. xxii + 890pp.
20100-7 Clothbound $8.50

THE EVOLUTION OF THE ENGLISH LANGUAGE, George McKnight. The growth of English, from the 14th century to the present. Unusual, non-technical account presents basic information in very interesting form: sound shifts, change in grammar and syntax, vocabulary growth, similar topics. Abundantly illustrated with quotations. Formerly Modern English in the Making. xii + 590pp.
21932-1 Paperbound $3.50

AN ETYMOLOGICAL DICTIONARY OF MODERN ENGLISH, Ernest Weekley. Fullest, richest work of its sort, by foremost British lexicographer. Detailed word histories, including many colloquial and archaic words; extensive quotations. Do not confuse this with the Concise Etymological Dictionary, which is much abridged. Total of xxvii + 830pp. 6½ x 9¼.
21873-2, 21874-0 Two volumes, Paperbound $6.00

FLATLAND: A ROMANCE OF MANY DIMENSIONS, E. A. Abbott. Classic of science-fiction explores ramifications of life in a two-dimensional world, and what happens when a three-dimensional being intrudes. Amusing reading, but also useful as introduction to thought about hyperspace. Introduction by Banesh Hoffmann. 16 illustrations. xx + 103pp.   20001-9 Paperbound $1.00

MATHEMATICAL PUZZLES FOR BEGINNERS AND ENTHUSIASTS, Geoffrey Mott-Smith. 189 puzzles from easy to difficult—involving arithmetic, logic, algebra, properties of digits, probability, etc.—for enjoyment and mental stimulus. Explanation of mathematical principles behind the puzzles. 135 illustrations. viii + 248pp.
20198-8 Paperbound $1.75

PAPER FOLDING FOR BEGINNERS, William D. Murray and Francis J. Rigney. Easiest book on the market, clearest instructions on making interesting, beautiful origami. Sail boats, cups, roosters, frogs that move legs, bonbon boxes, standing birds, etc. 40 projects; more than 275 diagrams and photographs. 94pp.
20713-7 Paperbound $1.00

TRICKS AND GAMES ON THE POOL TABLE, Fred Herrmann. 79 tricks and games—some solitaires, some for two or more players, some competitive games—to entertain you between formal games. Mystifying shots and throws, unusual caroms, tricks involving such props as cork, coins, a hat, etc. Formerly *Fun on the Pool Table*. 77 figures. 95pp.
21814-7 Paperbound $1.00

HAND SHADOWS TO BE THROWN UPON THE WALL: A SERIES OF NOVEL AND AMUSING FIGURES FORMED BY THE HAND, Henry Bursill. Delightful picturebook from great-grandfather's day shows how to make 18 different hand shadows: a bird that flies, duck that quacks, dog that wags his tail, camel, goose, deer, boy, turtle, etc. Only book of its sort. vi + 33pp. 6½ x 9¼.   21779-5 Paperbound $1.00

WHITTLING AND WOODCARVING, E. J. Tangerman. 18th printing of best book on market. "If you can cut a potato you can carve" toys and puzzles, chains, chessmen, caricatures, masks, frames, woodcut blocks, surface patterns, much more. Information on tools, woods, techniques. Also goes into serious wood sculpture from Middle Ages to present, East and West. 464 photos, figures. x + 293pp.
20965-2 Paperbound $2.00

HISTORY OF PHILOSOPHY, Julián Marias. Possibly the clearest, most easily followed, best planned, most useful one-volume history of philosophy on the market; neither skimpy nor overfull. Full details on system of every major philosopher and dozens of less important thinkers from pre-Socratics up to Existentialism and later. Strong on many European figures usually omitted. Has gone through dozens of editions in Europe. 1966 edition, translated by Stanley Appelbaum and Clarence Strowbridge. xviii + 505pp.   21739-6 Paperbound $3.00

YOGA: A SCIENTIFIC EVALUATION, Kovoor T. Behanan. Scientific but non-technical study of physiological results of yoga exercises; done under auspices of Yale U. Relations to Indian thought, to psychoanalysis, etc. 16 photos. xxiii + 270pp.
20505-3 Paperbound $2.50

Prices subject to change without notice.
Available at your book dealer or write for free catalogue to Dept. GI, Dover Publications, Inc., 180 Varick St., N. Y., N. Y. 10014. Dover publishes more than 150 books each year on science, elementary and advanced mathematics, biology, music, art, literary history, social sciences and other areas.